DynamoDB Cookbook

Over 90 hands-on recipes for design Internet-scalable
web and mobile applications with Amazon DynamoDB

Tanmay Deshpande

BIRMINGHAM - MUMBAI

DynamoDB Cookbook

First published: September 2015

Production reference: 1210915

Published by Packt Publishing Ltd.
Livery Place
35 Livery Street
Birmingham B3 2PB, UK.

ISBN 978-1-78439-375-5

www.packtpub.com

Credits

Author
Tanmay Deshpande

Reviewers
Sergio Alcantara
Kenny Ha
Volker Kueffel
Dr. Jun-young Kwak

Commissioning Editor
Pramila Balan

Acquisition Editor
Shaon Basu

Content Development Editor
Divij Kotian

Technical Editor
Naveenkumar Jain

Copy Editor
Rashmi Sawant

Project Coordinator
Neha Bhatnagar

Proofreader
Safis Editing

Indexer
Hemangini Bari

Production Coordinator
Komal Ramchandani

Cover Work
Komal Ramchandani

About the Author

Tanmay Deshpande is a Hadoop and big data evangelist. He currently works with Symantec Corporation as a senior software engineer in Pune, India. He has interests in a wide range of technologies, such as Hadoop, Hive, Pig, NoSQL databases, Mahout, Sqoop, Java, cloud computing, and so on. He has vast experience in application development in various domains, such as finance, telecom, manufacturing, security, and retail. He enjoys solving machine learning problems and likes to spend his time reading anything that he can get his hands on. He has a great interest in open source technologies and has been promoting them through his talks. He has been invited to various colleges to conduct brainstorming sessions with students on the latest technologies.

Before Symantec Corporation, he worked with Infosys, where he worked as the lead Big Data/ Cloud developer. He was a core team member of the Infosys Big Data Edge platform. Through his innovative thinking and dynamic leadership, he successfully completed various projects.

Before he wrote this book, he also authored two books, Mastering DynamoDB and Cloud Computing. He regularly blogs at http://hadooptutorials.co.in

Acknowledgments

This is the third book in a row for me, and I can't stop myself from imagining this to be real without my grandparents' love and care. I know that they are there somewhere and constantly blessing me with their best wishes all the time. I would like to dedicate this book to my grandparents, Late Mrs. Usha and Late Mr. Bhaskar Deshpande, Mrs. Malati and Late Mr. Madhukar Budukh.

I would like to thank my wife, Sneha, for standing beside me through thick and thin. She has been the source of inspiration and motivation to achieve bigger and better in life. I appreciate her patience to allow me to dedicate more time for this book and understanding what it means to me, without any complaints.

I would like to thank my mom, Mrs. Manisha Deshpande, my dad, Mr. Avinash Deshpande, and my brother, Sakalya, for encouraging me to follow my ambitions and for making me what I am today.

Above all, I would like thank the Almighty for giving me power to believe in my passion and pursue my dreams. This would not have been possible without the faith I have in him!

About the Reviewers

Sergio Alcantara has been building cloud-based platforms since the beginning of Amazon Web Services. Over the years, he has built the backend infrastructure for mobile and web applications that empowered GPS data, big data, and sports gaming. He has taken advantage of cloud computing to build highly reliable and scalable platforms.

Among his latest projects, there are several that use DynamoDB in different ways, but two of them use DynamoDB as their main and only database. In one project, he utilizes DynamoDB to store large quantities of data (big data), and in the other, he took advantage of DynamoDB's high scalability to satisfy the demands of high traffic social and sports betting pool applications.

He also created several open source libraries, all of which are listed in his GitHub profile (`https://github.com/serg-io`). The most notable of these libraries is backbone-dynamodb, which extends Backbone, a popular JavaScript library that allows the developer to store Backbone data models in DynamoDB.

Kenny Ha is currently working as a Senior Systems Architect at a local private company in San Diego. He is passionate about learning new technologies, especially about the mobile internet and data structures. He developed a passion for programming and data structures in the fall of 1992, at the University of California, San Diego (UCSD) and has been devoted to it ever since. Nowadays, he's intrigued with the entire mobile internet ecosystem and is trying to learn more about it.

All this is thanks to his childhood best friend, who advised him to switch his major from Electrical Engineering to Computer Science. He appreciates this advice till date and is very proud of his decision. His university years were all about learning and doing what interests him, which is programming, more than doing his required coursework. Throughout his career, he has designed scalable distributed enterprise systems with strong data structures and database concepts that he learnt in his university.

He has worked on many projects that involved distributed computing and processing. He realized that technology has evolved fairly rapidly, starting from the old CORBA days to the modern days of distributed service-oriented web services. He's currently involved with learning more advanced theoretical concepts related to computer science, in order to understand the theoretical concepts taught in universities and transform them into programmable implementation of working code, which includes mobile advancements. One of the exciting projects he has designed is a Global Positioning System project. He designed a hybrid database structure to manage the mobile GPS devices on golf carts and automobile industries. These hybrid database structures included a RDBMS and NoSQL(DynamoDB) to persist high-volume GPS coordinates in millions. He said that the most fun and exciting part of the project was a multi-threaded parallel Java program, which persisted data to DynamoDB while a Node.JS program projected the GPS coordinates on the web page to allow for the viewing of the golf carts traveling in real time.

The most important concept here is that the business requirements will always dictate the architectural designs of a system. Therefore, make sure to adopt the best practices of good software designs for effectiveness, efficiency, and user-friendliness. In the future, there will always be new innovative ecosystems that will disrupt the current technology and market trends, including the mobile Internet. We are definitely looking forward to these ecosystems being taught at universities.

You can visit http://oneglobalonline.com for more information on global technology and mobile market trends.

> I would like to thank Packt Publishing for giving me the opportunity to review the DynamoDB Cookbook. I'm very proud and feel fortunate to be a part of a great team of reviewers.

Volker Kueffel has been a software engineer and architect for almost two decades, and he has been developing software since he was a teenager. A physicist by trade, he has worked on large-scale data systems in various verticals of the software industry, spanning from online travel, mobile, and enterprise applications to online advertising. He has worked with a wide variety of AWS services for several years and introduced DynamoDB in one of his projects, which became the backbone of a large data collection system holding several terabytes of data. He is a native of Germany and currently lives with his family in San Francisco, California.

Dr. Jun-young Kwak is currently a senior software engineer (Backend) at Spokeo, Inc., where he is seeking practical means to apply Big Data-driven AI approaches to complex distributed systems. He received his PhD from the Department of Computer Science at the University of Southern California. He was one of the USC Annenberg Fellows. During his PhD tenure, he has done research on multi-agent decision making in sustainability, specifically focusing on multi-objective optimization in energy domains, sequential decision making under uncertainty, and human-agent interaction/negotiation. He was also a member of the Teamcore Research Group at USC led by Professor Milind Tambe. Before joining USC, he worked as a robotics programmer at Agent Dynamics, Inc. and was a visiting scholar at the Robotics Institute, Carnegie Mellon University in Pittsburgh. He was doing research on multi-agent coordination and control for unmanned systems, specifically, the ACCAST system (Advanced Command and Control of Autonomous System Teams) and the USAR (Urban Search And Rescue) projects. The ACCAST project was supported by DoD. He was mainly working with professors, Katia Sycara and Paul Scerri, at Intelligent Software Agents Lab, CMU RI. Before he started working, he did research on path planning and rough terrain navigation for his master's degree at CMU RI. This project was part of the Mars Technology Program supported by JPL, NASA. His research included planning algorithms under uncertainty, extending particle RRT, identifying the optimal vehicle models, and reducing the execution errors using various learning techniques. He worked with professor Reid Simmons.

www.PacktPub.com

Support files, eBooks, discount offers, and more

For support files and downloads related to your book, please visit www.PacktPub.com.

Did you know that Packt offers eBook versions of every book published, with PDF and ePub files available? You can upgrade to the eBook version at www.PacktPub.com and as a print book customer, you are entitled to a discount on the eBook copy. Get in touch with us at service@packtpub.com for more details.

At www.PacktPub.com, you can also read a collection of free technical articles, sign up for a range of free newsletters and receive exclusive discounts and offers on Packt books and eBooks.

https://www2.packtpub.com/books/subscription/packtlib

Do you need instant solutions to your IT questions? PacktLib is Packt's online digital book library. Here, you can search, access, and read Packt's entire library of books.

Why subscribe?

- Fully searchable across every book published by Packt
- Copy and paste, print, and bookmark content
- On demand and accessible via a web browser

Free access for Packt account holders

If you have an account with Packt at www.PacktPub.com, you can use this to access PacktLib today and view 9 entirely free books. Simply use your login credentials for immediate access.

Table of Contents

Preface	**v**
Chapter 1: Taking Your First Steps with DynamoDB	**1**
Introduction	1
Signing up to the DynamoDB console	2
Creating the DynamoDB table using the console	4
Loading data into the table using the console	9
Querying data using the DynamoDB console	11
Deleting the DynamoDB table using the console	15
Analyzing DynamoDB metric on CloudWatch	17
Downloading and setting up DynamoDB Local	21
Using DynamoDB Local JavaScript Shell	23
Setting up AWS Command Line Interface for DynamoDB	25
Setting up the Eclipse IDE	27
Chapter 2: Operating with DynamoDB Tables	**31**
Introduction	31
Creating a table using the AWS SDK for Java	32
Creating a table using the AWS SDK for .Net	34
Creating a table using the AWS SDK for PHP	35
Updating a table using the AWS SDK for Java	37
Updating a table using the AWS SDK for .Net	38
Updating a table using the AWS SDK for PHP	39
Listing tables using the AWS SDK for Java	39
Listing tables using the AWS SDK for .Net	40
Listing tables using the AWS SDK for PHP	41
Deleting a table using the AWS SDK for Java	42
Deleting a table using the AWS SDK for .Net	43
Deleting a table using the AWS SDK for PHP	44

Chapter 3: Manipulating DynamoDB Items — 47

Introduction	48
Putting an item into the DynamoDB table using the AWS SDK for Java	48
Putting an item into the DynamoDB table using the AWS SDK for .Net	50
Putting an item into the DynamoDB table using the AWS SDK for PHP	51
Getting an item from the DynamoDB table using the AWS SDK for Java	52
Getting an item from the DynamoDB table using the AWS SDK for .Net	52
Getting an item from the DynamoDB table using the AWS SDK for PHP	53
Updating an item in the DynamoDB table using the AWS SDK for Java	54
Updating an item in the DynamoDB table using the AWS SDK for .Net	56
Updating an item in the DynamoDB table using the AWS SDK for PHP	58
Deleting an item from the DynamoDB table using the AWS SDK for Java	60
Deleting an item from the DynamoDB table using the AWS SDK for .Net	62
Deleting an item from the DynamoDB table using the AWS SDK for PHP	63
Getting multiple items using the AWS SDK for Java	65
Getting multiple items using the AWS SDK for .Net	66
Getting multiple items using the AWS SDK for PHP	68
Batch write operations using the AWS SDK for Java	69
Batch write operations using the AWS SDK for .Net	70
Batch write operations using the AWS SDK for PHP	72

Chapter 4: Managing DynamoDB Indexes — 75

Introduction	76
Creating a DynamoDB table with a Global Secondary Index using the AWS SDK for Java	76
Creating a DynamoDB table with a Global Secondary Index using the AWS SDK for .Net	79
Creating a DynamoDB table with a Global Secondary Index using the AWS SDK for PHP	81
Querying a Global Secondary Index using the AWS SDK for Java	83
Querying a Global Secondary Index using the AWS SDK for .Net	84
Querying a Global Secondary Index using the AWS SDK for PHP	85
Creating a DynamoDB table with a Local Secondary Index using the AWS SDK for Java	86
Creating a DynamoDB table with a Local Secondary Index using the AWS SDK for .Net	88
Creating a DynamoDB table with a Local Secondary Index using the AWS SDK for PHP	91
Querying a Local Secondary Index using the AWS SDK for Java	93
Querying a Local Secondary Index using the AWS SDK for .Net	94

Querying a Local Secondary Index using the AWS SDK for PHP 95
Using a Global Secondary Index for quick lookups 96

**Chapter 5: Exploring Higher Level Programming Interfaces
for DynamoDB** 99
Introduction 100
Creating a data model for the DynamoDB item using the object
persistence model in Java 100
Putting items into the DynamoDB table using the object persistence
model in Java 102
Retrieving items from the DynamoDB table using the object persistence
model in Java 103
Creating a custom object for the DynamoDB table using the object
persistence model in Java 104
Querying items from the DynamoDB table using the object persistence
model in Java 106
Scanning items from the DynamoDB table using the object persistence
model in Java 108
Saving items into the DynamoDB table using the object persistence
model in .Net 109
Retrieving items from the DynamoDB table using the object persistence
model in .Net 111
Creating a custom object for the DynamoDB table using the object
persistence model in .Net 112
Querying items from the DynamoDB table using the object persistence
model in .Net 114
Scanning items from the DynamoDB table using the object persistence
model in .Net 115

Chapter 6: Securing DynamoDB 117
Introduction 117
Creating users using AWS IAM 118
Creating a DynamoDB full access group using AWS IAM 120
Creating a DynamoDB read-only group using AWS IAM 122
Validating the DynamoDB access controls using the AWS IAM policy
simulator 123
Creating the custom policy to allow the DynamoDB console access
using AWS IAM 125
Creating a fine-grained access control policy using AWS IAM 129
Implementing the client-side encryption for the DynamoDB data 131
Implementing the client-side masking for the DynamoDB data 134

Chapter 7: DynamoDB Best Practices   137
Introduction   137
Using a standalone cache for frequently accessed items   138
Using the AWS ElastiCache for frequently accessed items   140
Compressing large data before storing it in DynamoDB   142
Using AWS S3 for storing large items   145
Catching DynamoDB errors   147
Performing auto-retries on DynamoDB errors   148
Performing atomic transactions on DynamoDB tables   151
Performing asynchronous requests to DynamoDB   153

Chapter 8: Integrating DynamoDB with other AWS Services   155
Introduction   155
Importing data from AWS S3 to DynamoDB using AWS Data Pipeline   156
Exporting data from AWS S3 to DynamoDB using AWS Data Pipeline   159
Accessing the DynamoDB data using AWS EMR   163
Querying the DynamoDB data using AWS EMR   167
Performing join operations on the DynamoDB data using AWS EMR   171
Exporting data to AWS S3 from DynamoDB using AWS EMR   172
Logging DynamoDB operations using AWS CloudTrail   174
Exporting the DynamoDB data to AWS Redshift   176
Importing the DynamoDB data to AWS CloudSearch   181
Performing a full text search on the DynamoDB data using CloudSearch   185

Chapter 9: Developing Web Applications using DynamoDB   189
Introduction   189
Performing data modeling and table creations   190
Developing services for the sign-up activity for web applications   193
Developing services for the sign-in activity for web applications   198
Developing services for the Address Book application   200
Deploying web applications on AWS Elastic Beanstalk   206

Chapter 10: Developing Mobile Applications using DynamoDB   215
Introduction   215
Performing data modeling and table creation   216
Creating an identity pool using AWS Cognito   219
Creating the access policy and applying it to the AWS Cognito role   222
Implementing user registration services   224
Implementing user login services   227
Implementing add new contact services   230
Implementing view contacts services   234

Index   237

Preface

AWS DynamoDB is an excellent example of a production-ready NoSQL database. In recent years, DynamoDB has been able to attract many customers because of its features, such as high-availability, reliability, and infinite scalability. DynamoDB can be easily integrated with massive data crunching tools such as Hadoop/EMR, which is an essential part of this data-driven world, and hence, it is widely accepted. The cost and time efficient design makes DynamoDB stand out differently among its peers. The design of DynamoDB is so neat and clean that it has inspired many NoSQL databases to simply follow it.

This book is a practical, example-oriented guide that starts with simple recipes, such as how to get started with creating a DynamoDB table, and gradually takes you through the advanced level recipes, such as how to create Internet scalable web/mobile applications using DynamoDB as a backend. It explains recipes on how to integrate DynamoDB with other AWS services such as AWS EMR, AWS CloudSearch, AWS Redshift, and many others. It also contains various recipes on how to secure DynamoDB using AWS IAM. It has plenty of recipes that discuss the DynamoDB best practices, which will help you use DynamoDB in the most efficient manner. It is concise with clean topic descriptions, plenty of screenshots, and code samples in order to enhance the clarity and to help you try and test things on your own.

What this book covers

Chapter 1, Taking Your First Steps with DynamoDB, introduces you to the DynamoDB console, AWS CLI, and DynamoDB Local, and you will learn simple CRUD operations on a DynamoDB table. It also covers how to set up your workspace to perform various recipes in the later chapters.

Chapter 2, Operating with DynamoDB Tables, provides you with hands-on recipes that can be performed on DynamoDB tables using the AWS SDK for Java, .NET, and PHP, along with a detailed explanation.

Chapter 3, Manipulating DynamoDB Items, enlightens you with various recipes on DynamoDB and how to manipulate DynamoDB items. Recipes that discuss batch, get, and write operations will help you understand how to handle bulk data in a cost efficient manner.

Chapter 4, Managing DynamoDB Indexes, helps you understand the use of secondary indexes in detail. It gives you ready-to-cook recipes on how to use Global and Local secondary indexes using the AWS SDK for Java, .NET, and PHP.

Chapter 5, Exploring High Level Programming Interfaces for DynamoDB, covers topics, such as object persistence model interfaces provided by the AWS SDK for Java and .NET. A detailed explanation on annotation-driven APIs is also provided in this chapter.

Chapter 6, Securing DynamoDB, introduces you to a rich identity and access model provided by AWS and how to apply that to DynamoDB. Recipes, such as client-side encryption and masking, are helpful to achieve high-level security for data stored in DynamoDB.

Chapter 7, DynamoDB Best Practices, covers various recipes on the cost and performance efficient services used in DynamoDB. Recipes, such as error handling and auto retries, will help you make your application robust. It also highlights the use of a transaction library in order to implement atomic transactions on DynamoDB.

Chapter 8, Integrating DynamoDB with other AWS Services, provides you ready-to-use recipes of how to integrate DynamoDB with various other AWS services, such as AWS Pipeline, EMR, S3, CloudSearch, Redshift, and so on. You will also learn when to integrate with which service.

Chapter 9, Developing Web Applications using DynamoDB, gives you an end-to-end experience on how to create web applications using DynamoDB as a database. At the end of this chapter, you will not only learn how to start, but also how to deploy the application on AWS Elastic Beanstalk.

Chapter 10, Developing Mobile Applications using DynamoDB, discusses how to build an Internet scalable mobile application using DynamoDB as a database. It also helps you understand how to use Asynchronous calls while accessing DynamoDB from Android apps.

What you need for this book

To get started with this book, you should have a laptop/desktop with any OS, such as Windows, UNIX, or Mac. You should have an Internet connection to access DynamoDB. It's also good to have the development IDE, such as Eclipse or Visual Studio.

Who this book is for

This book is intended for those who have a basic understanding of AWS services and want to take their knowledge to the next level by getting their hands dirty with coding recipes in DynamoDB.

Sections

In this book, you will find several headings that appear frequently (Getting ready, How to do it, How it works, There's more, and See also).

To give clear instructions on how to complete a recipe, we use these sections as follows:

Getting ready

This section tells you what to expect in the recipe, and describes how to set up any software or any preliminary settings required for the recipe.

How to do it...

This section contains the steps required to follow the recipe.

How it works...

This section usually consists of a detailed explanation of what happened in the previous section.

There's more...

This section consists of additional information about the recipe in order to make the reader more knowledgeable about the recipe.

See also

This section provides helpful links to other useful information for the recipe.

Conventions

In this book, you will find a number of text styles that distinguish between different kinds of information. Here are some examples of these styles and an explanation of their meaning.

Code words in text, database table names, folder names, filenames, file extensions, pathnames, dummy URLs, user input, and Twitter handles are shown as follows: "We can include other contexts through the use of the `include` directive."

A block of code is set as follows:

```
<dependency>
  <groupId>com.amazonaws</groupId>
  <artifactId>aws-java-sdk</artifactId>
  <version>1.9.30</version>
</dependency>
```

Any command-line input or output is written as follows:

```
aws dynamodb query --table-name product --key-conditions file://
conditions.json
```

New terms and **important words** are shown in bold. Words that you see on the screen, for example, in menus or dialog boxes, appear in the text like this: "Click on the **Sign in to the Console** button."

 Warnings or important notes appear in a box like this.

 Tips and tricks appear like this.

Reader feedback

Feedback from our readers is always welcome. Let us know what you think about this book—what you liked or disliked. Reader feedback is important for us as it helps us develop titles that you will really get the most out of.

To send us general feedback, simply e-mail feedback@packtpub.com, and mention the book's title in the subject of your message.

If there is a topic that you have expertise in and you are interested in either writing or contributing to a book, see our author guide at www.packtpub.com/authors.

Customer support

Now that you are the proud owner of a Packt book, we have a number of things to help you to get the most from your purchase.

Downloading the example code

You can download the example code files from your account at `http://www.packtpub.com` for all the Packt Publishing books you have purchased. If you purchased this book elsewhere, you can visit `http://www.packtpub.com/support` and register to have the files e-mailed directly to you.

Downloading the color images of this book

We also provide you with a PDF file that has color images of the screenshots/diagrams used in this book. The color images will help you better understand the changes in the output. You can download this file from `http://www.packtpub.com/sites/default/files/downloads/36590S_ColorImages.pdf`.

Errata

Although we have taken every care to ensure the accuracy of our content, mistakes do happen. If you find a mistake in one of our books—maybe a mistake in the text or the code—we would be grateful if you could report this to us. By doing so, you can save other readers from frustration and help us improve subsequent versions of this book. If you find any errata, please report them by visiting `http://www.packtpub.com/submit-errata`, selecting your book, clicking on the **Errata Submission Form** link, and entering the details of your errata. Once your errata are verified, your submission will be accepted and the errata will be uploaded to our website or added to any list of existing errata under the Errata section of that title.

To view the previously submitted errata, go to `https://www.packtpub.com/books/content/support` and enter the name of the book in the search field. The required information will appear under the **Errata** section.

Piracy

Piracy of copyrighted material on the Internet is an ongoing problem across all media. At Packt, we take the protection of our copyright and licenses very seriously. If you come across any illegal copies of our works in any form on the Internet, please provide us with the location address or website name immediately so that we can pursue a remedy.

Please contact us at `copyright@packtpub.com` with a link to the suspected pirated material.

We appreciate your help in protecting our authors and our ability to bring you valuable content.

Questions

If you have a problem with any aspect of this book, you can contact us at questions@
packtpub.com, and we will do our best to address the problem.

1
Taking Your First Steps with DynamoDB

In this chapter, we will cover the following topics:

- ► Signing up to the DynamoDB console
- ► Creating the DynamoDB table using the console
- ► Loading data into the table using the console
- ► Querying data using the DynamoDB console
- ► Deleting the DynamoDB table using the console
- ► Analyzing DynamoDB metric on CloudWatch
- ► Downloading and setting up DynamoDB Local
- ► Using DynamoDB Local JavaScript Shell
- ► Setting up AWS Command Line Interface for DynamoDB
- ► Setting up the Eclipse IDE

Introduction

Amazon DynamoDB is a fully managed and cloud-hosted NoSQL database. NoSQL databases allow us to have a schema-less design for the tables. We only need to define the key, and the rest of the attributes can be defined at the time of record insertion itself.

DynamoDB provides a fast and predictable performance with the ability to scale seamlessly. It allows you to store and retrieve any amount of data, serving any level of network traffic without having any operational burden. DynamoDB gives numerous other advantages, such as a consistent and predictable performance, flexible data modelling, and durability. This chapter is all about taking your first steps with DynamoDB, getting your workspace ready, and seeing how to perform DynamoDB operations using the DynamoDB console. Now let's get started with the sign up process.

Signing up to the DynamoDB console

To get started with DynamoDB, we need to first create an account with Amazon Web Services.

Getting ready

AWS provides an interactive console to perform the **Sign Up** process. Being a pay-as-you-go model, we need to provide valid credit card details while registering. AWS also needs a valid phone, which is verified at the time of registration itself. So, you need to keep both the things handy.

How to do it...

Let's get started with DynamoDB:

1. To sign in to the AWS Console, go to `http://aws.amazon.com/`.

2. Click on the **Sign in to the Console** button:

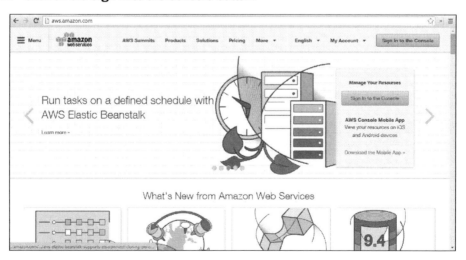

3. To begin with the sign up process, follow the onscreen instructions by providing the valid e-mail address.

4. Enter all the details asked correctly, and click on the **Press Create Account** button:

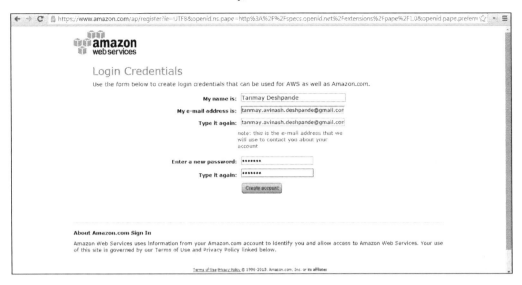

5. In the next screen, you would need to provide the contact information, and later, capture the billing information by providing the credit card information.

6. The last step would be to provide your phone number. AWS calls the provided phone number, and you are supposed to enter the on screen PIN number on your phone dial pad. Once you are done, you will see the **AWS Management** console.

7. Now, you can select the **DynamoDB** service under the **Database** section to go to the DynamoDB console:

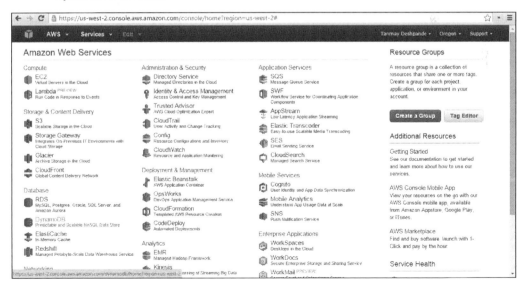

8. That's it! You are all set to use DynamoDB.

How it works...

AWS manages the accounts created through its console, and allows the user to access it over defined authentication methods. For any new account, AWS provides the free tier up to a certain threshold. You can read more about this at `http://docs.aws.amazon.com/awsaccountbilling/latest/aboutv2/billing-free-tier.html`.

There's more...

Note that on registration, AWS charges you 1 USD for the verification of your credit card, but the payment gets reversed after some days. You may take a look at the **AWS Billing FAQs** for more details at `http://aws.amazon.com/billing/faqs/`.

Creating the DynamoDB table using the console

Now that we have signed up for AWS, let's start by creating our first DynamoDB table using the DynamoDB console.

Getting ready

To perform this recipe, you need to have completed the earlier recipe of *Signing up to the DynamoDB AWS console*.

How to do it...

Let's create our first DynamoDB table. The steps are as follows:

1. Sign in to the **AWS Console** by providing valid account details, and go to the DynamoDB console, as shown in the previous recipe. You will see the following screen:

2. Click on the **Create Table** button. This will open a popup window where you will need to provide details, such as the **Table Name**, **Primary Key**, their data types, and so on. Here, we need to create a table called a `product` table, which will save the products-related data for all the e-commerce websites.

Here, we will create a table with the **Primary Key Type** as the **Hash and Range** composite keys. We will have the `hash key` as the product `id` and `range key` as the product `type`. Add the details, as shown in the following screenshot, and click on **Continue**:

3. In the next screen, you need to add `Global/Local Secondary Indexes`. Here, we would like to query DynamoDB items with their `name` and `manufacturer`. So, we create an index, and click on the **Add Index to Table** button, as shown in the following screenshot. Once done, click on **Continue** to proceed with the next configuration:

Here, we are also selecting **Projected Attributes** as **All Attributes**, as we would like DynamoDB to give us all the attributes back when we query it. Alternatively, if you know exactly what attributes you need to be projected into this secondary index, you can select **Specify Attributes**, in the **Projected Attributes** dropdown, and add the specific attributes you want to be projected.

4. Provide **Read Capacity Units** and **Write Capacity Units**, depending on the reads and writes load you are expecting. Here, I am providing the value **5** for **Read Capacity Units** and **5** for **Write Capacity Units**, as shown in the following screenshot. Click on the **Continue** button to proceed. A read capacity unit is a strong consistent read per second for items as large as 4 KB, while a write capacity unit is a strong consistent write per second for items as large as 1 KB:

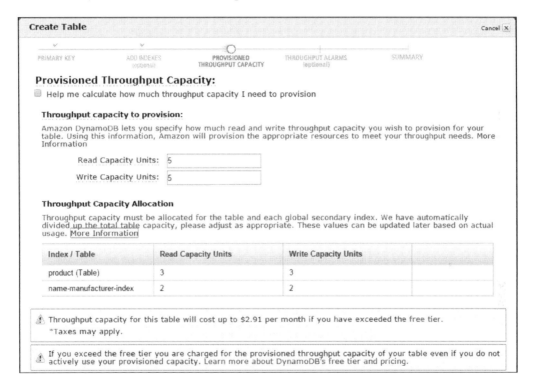

5. The next screen will be all about setting up the throughput alarms. Here, you can select the checkbox for when you wish to get alarms in case your throughput reaches capacity. This is an optional configuration, so you may wish to skip it. Click on **Continue** to move to the next step.

6. The last step is to review the summary. If you are okay with the configurations, then click on **Create** to actually create the DynamoDB table. If you think that there are some configurations that are missing, then you may wish to go back and change those.

7. The newly created DynamoDB table may take some time to get active; in the meantime, you will see **Status** as **Creating** on the screen.

8. Lastly, you will see that the table is created and is in the **ACTIVE** state:

How it works...

In DynamoDB, we don't need to bother about the availability, scalability, and reliability of the table as it is completely owned by Amazon. We just need to create a table and start using it. We can modify the throughput units any time using the same console. This gives us the flexibility to control the reads and writes of the data from DynamoDB. For example, if you think that there is a certain period where you would be expecting more reads/writes, then you can increase the throughput values and vice versa. You can find out how AWS calculates the read and write throughput at

```
http://docs.aws.amazon.com/amazondynamodb/latest/developerguide/
ProvisionedThroughputIntro.html.
```

Choosing a right key is very important in order to balance the load on DynamoDB partitions. The hash key should be chosen in such a way that it has unique values in it so that the data can be distributed across the cluster. The range key should be chosen in such a way that items can be grouped together so that if you have any such queries, they will perform faster. This is why we have chosen the product **id** as the **Hash Key** attribute, while the product **type** as the **Range Key** attribute.

The same is the case with **Global Secondary Indexes**. The Global secondary indexes allow us to query items on non-primary key attributes. Here, we may want to query items on their names or group them by the manufacturer.

DynamoDB supports various data types for its attributes, which are as follows:

- **Scalar**: Number, String, Binary, Boolean, and Null
- **Multi-valued**: String Set, Number Set, and Binary Set
- **Document**: List and Map

You can choose which suites you best.

There's more...

Here, you might have noticed that instead of putting the manufacturer's name as a proper name to the range key in the **Global Secondary Index**, I chose to use its short form as `mnfr`. The reason for this is that when it comes to key-value pair types of databases, the entries stored in the database are always both keys and values together. So, every time you add an item or an attribute, it will be saved as `key=value` in the database. So, it's the best practice to use short yet meaningful names for keys and attributes. We will discuss such best practices in *Chapter 7, DynamoDB Best Practices*.

Loading data into the table using the console

We were able to create a table in DynamoDB in the previous recipe; now, we will load the data into that table using the console.

Getting ready

To perform this recipe, you need to have completed the earlier recipe of *Creating the DynamoDB table using the console*.

How to do it...

Let's load the data into the table:

1. Select the table in which you wish to load the data into the console, and click on the **Explore Table** button.

2. As we have not added any items to the table yet, it will show No Items Found on your screen, as shown in the following screenshot:

3. Click on the **Create Item** button to add a new item to the table. By default, it opens the **Put Item** screen in the **Tree** mode, where you can add values and the keys. You can also add more attributes to the item based on the requirements, as shown in the following screenshot:

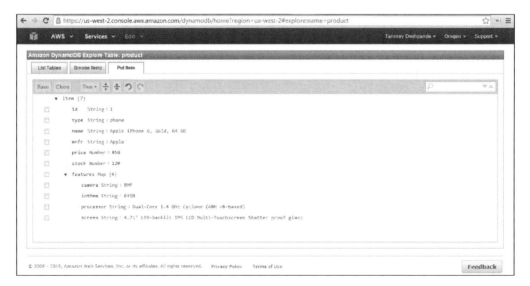

4. Click on the **Save** button to add an item to the table.
5. Repeat the earlier mentioned steps to add more items to the table.

How it works...

This simply adds the items against the DynamoDB table that we created. DynamoDB supports various data types, such as `String`, `Number`, `Binary`, `String Set`, `Number Set`, `Map`, `List`, `Boolean`, and `Null`. You can choose the correct data type that is suitable for the operations you would need to perform.

You can refer to the documentation for more details at `http://docs.aws.amazon.com/amazondynamodb/latest/developerguide/DataModel.html#DataModel.DataTypes`.

Querying data using the DynamoDB console

In the earlier recipe, we learned how to add new items to the DynamoDB table. In this recipe, we will learn how to query the data that is added using the DynamoDB console.

Getting ready

To perform this recipe, you need to have completed the earlier recipe to add items to the DynamoDB table.

How to do it...

Let's perform different types of queries on AWS DynamoDB console:

1. To perform the various types of queries, we will first need to go to the AWS DynamoDB console, select the table against which we would like to execute our queries, and then click on the **Explore Table** button. This will execute a scan operation on the selected table, which will look like this:

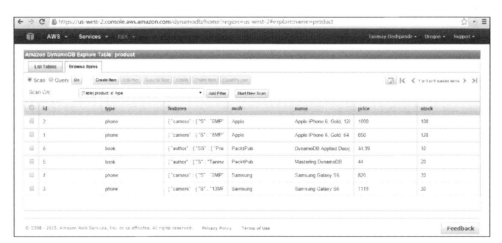

2. Now, to perform a query operation, select the **Query** radio button. In the dropdown below it, you will see a choice to perform the query either on the table indexes or secondary indexes, which were created earlier. The first query we will perform will be to get the item by its **id**. Here, if you want to fetch an item/s whose `id` is 1, put 1 in the `textbox` against the **Hash Key**, click on the **Query** button, and you will see the results immediately:

3. We can also query data by providing a combination of **Hash Key** and **Range Key** to narrow down our search. In the earlier scenario, we got two items: one with the type `phone`, and another with the type `book`. Now if we want to fetch the item whose `id` is 1 and the type is `phone`, then we can query that accordingly, and we will get the results as required:

4. We can also query data on the **Global Secondary Index**, which we created at the time of table creation:

5. Similarly, we can use the `scan` operations in order to fetch the data from the DynamoDB table. We can either do a complete scan or a filtered scan. To perform a complete table scan, we have to select the **Scan** radio button, and click on the **Start New Scan** button. As we have not put any filters on the scan, this operation will fetch all the items present in the given DynamoDB table:

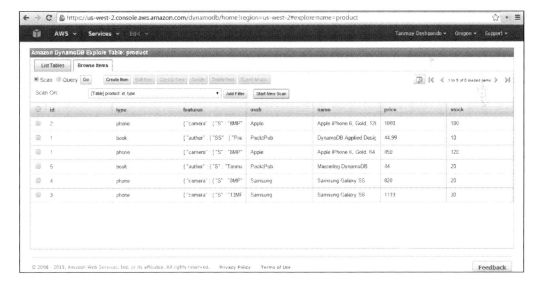

6. We can also add filters to the scan operation by clicking on the **Add Filter** button, and then by providing the filtering criteria. For example, if we want to fetch all the items of the phone type, then we can specify the criteria, and execute the scan operation.

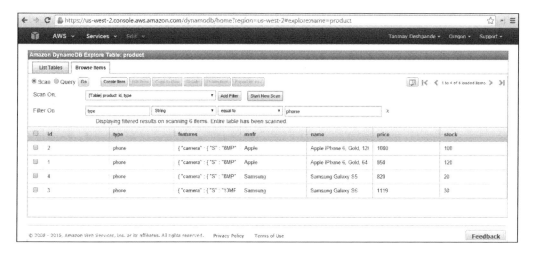

7. Scan filters allow comparison operations, such as equal to, less than, less than or equal to, greater than, greater than or equal to, null, not null, contains, not contain, begins with, and so on. You can use it as per your need. Scan filtering can also be performed on the global secondary index. For example, if we want to fetch all the items whose manufacture name starts with A, then we can add this filter and get the results:

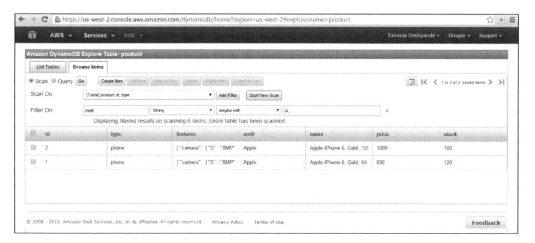

How it works...

Query and **Scan** are powerful operations that help us to retrieve data. However, both have their own working style and their own pros and cons.

A `Query` operation finds items in the table using the primary key attributes. You can specify the hash key and optional range key in order to get the desired items. By default, a Query operation returns all the attributes of a given item, but there is an option available to limit the attributes using `ProjectionExpressions`. While providing the key conditions, the Query operation expects an equality condition on the Hash Key attribute, but there are a set of conditions allowed to specify the Range Key conditions.

A query request can retrieve a maximum of **1 MB** of data at a time. So, you need to plan the Query operation accordingly. You can optionally use `FilterExpressions` to narrow down this data. The Hash Key index is an unordered index, which means that we can only specify an exact key to fetch the items, whereas the Range Key index is an ordered index, which allows us to query that index using various `ConditionalOperations`, such as less than, greater than, begins with, between, and so on. If no matches are found, Query returns an empty result set.

A Scan operation examines each and every item in the given DynamoDB table, compares it with the condition, and gets the results back. By default, this also returns all the attributes of the items back to the user. Of course, we can use `ProjectionExpressions` to limit the set of attributes returned by the scan request.

A single scan request can fetch a maximum of **1 MB** of data. To make the best use of it, we can also use `FilterExpressions` to narrow down the result set.

There are ways to handle this limitation of **1 MB** of data per request, but we cannot do much using the DynamoDB console, so we will talk about all these details in *Chapter 2, Operating with DynamoDB Tables*.

Deleting the DynamoDB table using the console

In the earlier recipe, we discussed using the Query and Scan operations on the DynamoDB table using the console. Now, we will see how to delete a table using the same.

Getting ready

To perform this recipe, you need to create a table. Please create a dummy table, say `dummyProduct`, in DynamoDB using the recipe *Creating the DynamoDB table using the console*.

How to do it...

Note that by performing the following set of operations, the table and its data will get deleted forever, and there is no way to get it back, so I would suggest that you perform this recipe only if you know that the table is not needed anymore:

1. Here, I have two tables in my DynamoDB console now, out of which I will delete a table called `dummyProduct`:

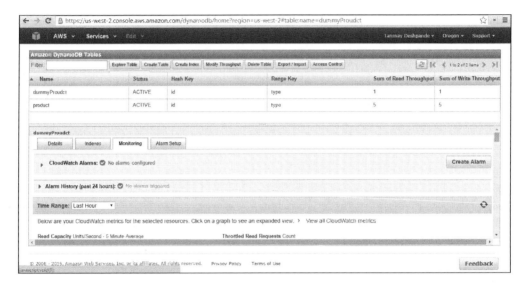

2. Select a table to be deleted, and click on the **Delete Table** button:

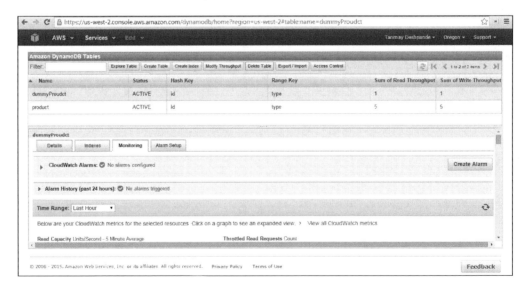

3. This will open up a pop-up window, which will ask you for your confirmation. Check the checkbox against the **Delete this table** text, and click on the **Delete** button:

4. This will start the deleting process, which will run for a while and erase the complete data.

How it works...

The delete operation completely erases the data in the given table and drops that table from DynamoDB. If you delete the DynamoDB table, there is no way to get that data back, so perform this operation very carefully. I would suggest that you avoid this operation if you don't know the criticality of this table.

Analyzing DynamoDB metric on CloudWatch

It is very important to keep an eye on DynamoDB CloudWatch metrics in order to see the DynamoDB performance. CloudWatch provides real-time monitoring and alerting mechanisms to services provided by DynamoDB.

Getting ready

To get a better understanding of DynamoDB metrics, considering the fact that we don't have much of our data in our product table, go to the Query and Scan operations console and perform various Query and Scan operations back to back in order to get some metrics. Simply clicking on the **Query** and **Scan** buttons with some sample conditions will do the job for you.

Of course, in real time, in production systems, you would not need to do this as we will automatically have sufficient reads, writes, queries, and scans in progress.

How to do it...

Let's understand DynamoDB metrics on Cloudwatch:

1. Go to the DynamoDB console, and click on the table whose metrics you would like to analyze. You will notice that the bottom frame will start showing some details about the table. It will have various tabs, such as **Details**, which will have the table details, **Indexes**, which will have details about the secondary indexes that we created in our table, **Monitoring**, which will have the details about the CloudWatch metrics that we would like to see in detail, and the last tab, **Alarm Setup**, which is used to set up various alarms in case you wish to get any:

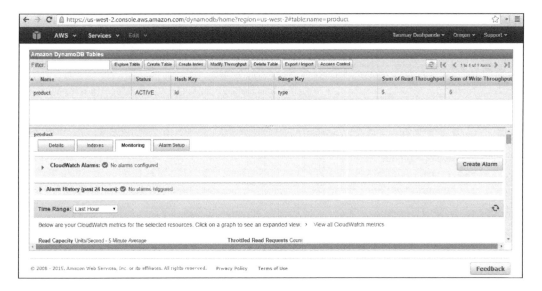

2. If you scroll down a bit, you will see various graphs, such as Read Capacity, Throttled Read Requests, Write Capacity, Throttled Write Requests, Read-Write Capacity for Global Secondary Indexes, that we created. It will also show you graphs related to Read/Write Latency and Query/Scan latency for a given time frame:

3. You can also click on individual graphs to see the enlarged view. I have made a significant number of scans in the last hour; if I want to see how DynamoDB performed for a particular time frame, I need to click on the Scan Latency graph, which will open the enlarged view of the graph, as shown in the following screenshot:

The preceding graph tells us the average time taken by DynamoDB in milliseconds to perform the various scan operations.

4. You can also change the Statistic drop-down value to select the various metrics. For example, if I want to see the exact time taken by each scan request over the last hour, it will show you the results immediately. I can also click on the data points on the graph to see the exact time. Here is an example of it:

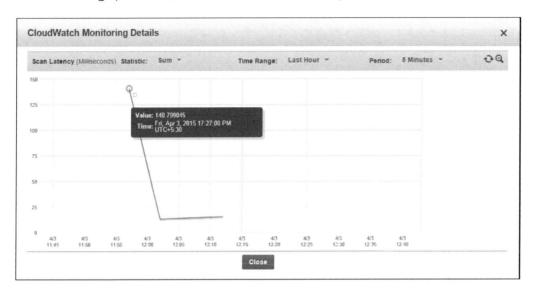

Here, the graph tells us that the very first scan request took approximately 140 milliseconds to fetch the results, whereas the latency dropped in subsequent requests, and eventually, improved the performance.

How it works...

Almost every operation in Cloud is measured in terms of bytes read/written. CloudWatch keeps track of the requests that we make to DynamoDB and stores it in the internal data store. While generating the graphs, we will use these data points, which will help us analyze the performance.

There's more...

You can also analyze other CloudWatch metrics to better understand the DynamoDB behavior. These graphs will also help you decide upon the throughput values set for the tables and secondary indexes. If you see the consumed read/write capacity reaching the provisioned read/write capacity, then you can increase the provisioned throughput and vice versa.

Always look for consistent metrics; you might miss out on certain spikes because a lot of graphs give you an average of values over the last 5 minutes of time. For more detailed metrics, you can go to the CloudWatch console and look out for DynamoDB metrics at `https://console.aws.amazon.com/cloudwatch/https://console.aws.amazon.com/cloudwatch/`.

Downloading and setting up DynamoDB Local

A call to any cloud resource may cost money to you, even if you are just doing development and not talking about any hosting in the production cluster. During development, we may need to try many things, and all those trials would cost us. The development best practices demand us to follow a test-driven development. For continuous integration and builds, it's good to run unit tests and integration tests to make sure that the build is intact. If we keep running unit tests and integration tests on the actual DynamoDB, we may end up paying a lot. To cater to this issue, we have something called as DynamoDB Local.

DynamoDB Local is a small client-side database and server that mimics the actual DynamoDB. It enables you to develop and test your code in the local environment, without modifying anything on the actual DynamoDB. It is compatible with the actual DynamoDB API, so there is no need to worry about duplicating your efforts.

Getting ready

DynamoDB Local is a **Java Archive** (**JAR**) file, which will run on the Windows, Mac, or Linux machines. To execute these APIs, you should have **Java Runtime Engine** (**JRE**) 6.0+ installed on your machine. You can refer to following docs to install JRE on your machine:

For Windows 64-bit machine: `http://www.oracle.com/technetwork/java/javase/install-windows-64-142952.html`.

For Windows 32-bit machine: `http://www.oracle.com/technetwork/java/javase/install-windows-141940.html`.

For Mac: `http://docs.oracle.com/javase/7/docs/webnotes/install/mac/mac-jre.html`.

How to do it...

You can download DynamoDB Local from the following locations:

- **tar.gz format**: `http://dynamodb-local.s3-website-us-west-2.amazonaws.com/dynamodb_local_latest.tar.gz`
- **.zip format**: `http://dynamodb-local.s3-website-us-west-2.amazonaws.com/dynamodb_local_latest.zip`

Now, let's perform the following steps to install DynamoDB Local:

1. Once done, just unzip the `.jar` file, and save it in a folder.

2. Now use Command Prompt, go to the folder where you have unzipped the `.jar` file, and execute the following command:

```
java -Djava.library.path=./DynamoDBLocal_lib -jar DynamoDBLocal.
jar
```

You will see the jetty server getting started at `http://localhost:8000`:

3. Now you can use this as an endpoint for your development. For example, if we want to use it in the Java SDK, we can use this as follows:

```
client = new AmazonDynamoDBClient(credentials);
client.setEndpoint("http://localhost:8000");
```

We will see more of its uses in the following chapters.

How it works...

DynamoDB Local is a simple `.jar` file that runs on your local machine and mimics the actual DynamoDB. You can do your development using DynamoDB, test your code, and simply redirect to the actual DynamoDB whenever it is ready for production deployment. Even though DynamoDB Local mimics most of the DynamoDB features, it does not support some important ones, which are as follows:

- ▶ It does not consider the provisioned throughput settings while making any calls.
- ▶ It does not throttle the read or write activity. The `CreateTable`, `UpdateTable`, and `DeleteTable` operations occur immediately. The table state is always **ACTIVE**.
- ▶ It does not keep track of the consumed capacity units. So, it always returns null instead of the actual capacity units.
- ▶ Read operations in DynamoDB are eventually consistent, but due to the speed of DynamoDB Local, it appears to be strongly consistent.

There's more...

The DynamoDB Local .jar gives you various other options in addition in order to manage DynamoDB Local smoothly. Here are some more options:

The -help function will list all the options available with DynamoDB Local JAR, as shown in the following command:

```
java -Djava.library.path=./DynamoDBLocal_lib -jar DynamoDBLocal.jar -
help
```

The output is shown in the following command:

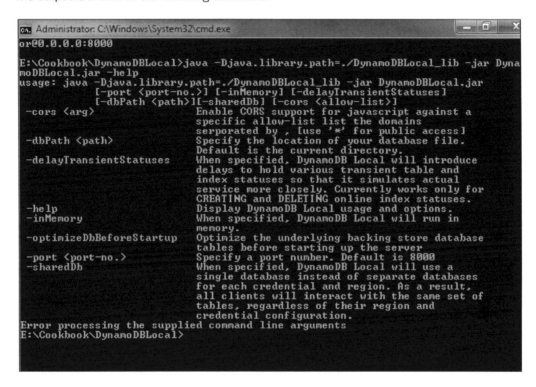

Using DynamoDB Local JavaScript Shell

With the latest version of DynamoDB Local, you can also get an interactive DynamoDB Local JavaScript shell. In this recipe, we are going to see how to use it.

Getting ready

To perform this recipe, you need to have completed the earlier recipe of *Downloading and setting up DynamoDB Local*.

How to do it...

Enabling DynamoDB Local does not require any extra effort; we need to simply start DynamoDB Local, and go to `http://localhost:8000/shell/` in the browser of your choice - you will see the interactive shell:

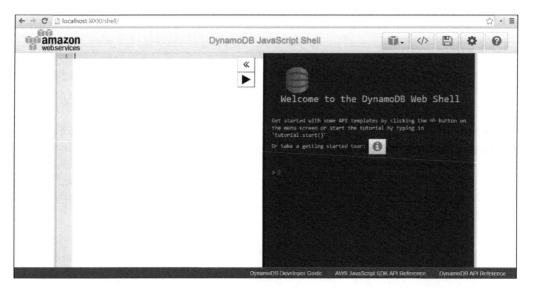

This interesting hands-on tutorial will help you understand DynamoDB. At the end of this tutorial, you will be able to create certain tables, try out various item levels and operations, and also create a demo application. Just use the navigation options as directed and this will be done.

How it works...

This DynamoDB Local Shell application runs using a regular application server and code in Java/JavaScript. This gets more interesting as you will actually get to do many things using DynamoDB JavaScript commands.

Setting up AWS Command Line Interface for DynamoDB

The AWS Command Line Interface allows us to operate various AWS resources from the command line itself. In this recipe, we are going to see how to use these and perform operations.

Getting ready

You can download the installer for Windows, Mac, or Linux from `http://aws.amazon.com/cli/`.

How to do it...

The AWS CLI for DynamoDB supports various commands, such as batch-get-item, batch-write-item, create-table, delete-item, delete-table, describe-table, get-item, list-tables, put-item, query, scan, update-item, update-table, wait, and so on.

To get started, we need to first configure the AWS CLI:

1. Start Command Prompt, and type the following command:

    `aws configure`

2. This will ask you for the `Access Key`, `Secret Key`, and `Region` details. If you have not downloaded the AWS keys yet, you can download them from `https://console.aws.amazon.com/iam/home?#security_credential`.

3. Here, you can download the `Access Keys` and save it in a secure place. Once the keys are submitted, you can start accessing DynamoDB from the command line.

4. We need to list the tables that we have already created, and then we can execute this command:

    `aws dynamodb list-tables`

    The output of the following command is shown below:

```
C:\Users\TDeshpande>aws dynamodb list-tables
{
    "TableNames": [
        "product"
    ]
}

C:\Users\TDeshpande>
```

5. We can also run the `Query` operations from the command line as well. Suppose that we want to Query a product table for `id =5`, then we have to write this condition in the JSON document and save it on our machine. The JSON file would like this:

```
{"id": {"AttributeValueList": [{"S":"5"}],"ComparisonOperator": "EQ" }}
```

Assume that we saved it in a file named `conditions.json`; then, to execute the query, we have to run the following command:

```
aws dynamodb query --table-name product --key-conditions file://
conditions.json
```

The output would be something like this:

```
C:\Users\TDeshpande>aws dynamodb query --table-name product --key-conditions fil
e://conditions.json
{
    "Count": 1,
    "Items": [
        {
            "mnfr": {
                "S": "PacktPub"
            },
            "features": {
                "M": {
                    "paperback": {
                        "S": "230 Pages"
                    },
                    "ISBN": {
                        "S": "978-1783551958"
                    },
                    "dimensions": {
                        "S": "7.5 x 0.5 x 9.2 inches"
                    },
                    "author": {
                        "S": "Tanmay Deshpande"
                    }
                }
            },
            "price": {
                "N": "44"
            },
            "name": {
                "S": "Mastering DynamoDB"
            },
            "type": {
                "S": "book"
            },
            "id": {
                "S": "5"
            },
            "stock": {
                "N": "20"
            }
        }
    ],
    "ScannedCount": 1,
    "ConsumedCapacity": null
}
```

We can also specify conditions for the Range Key in order to narrow down our results, which is similar to what we did for the Hash Key.

How it works...

The AWS CLI, which is internally called DynamoDB APIs, is used to retrieve results. For authentication, it uses the Access Key and Secret Key that you provide at the time of configuration.

There's more...

You can also try out various other options from the AWS CLI for DynamoDB, which are available at `http://docs.aws.amazon.com/cli/latest/reference/dynamodb/index.html#cli-aws-dynamodb`.

Setting up the Eclipse IDE

Eclipse is an IDE, which is used mostly for Java development. In order to avoid switching screens between Eclipse and your browser, you can simply install the AWS plugin for Eclipse. In this recipe, we are going to see how to set up this plugin, and how to use it to perform various DynamoDB operations.

Getting ready

The first thing you need to do is install Eclipse on your laptop/desktop. The latest version from Eclipse can be downloaded from `https://eclipse.org/downloads/`. You need to select the Eclipse IDE for Java developers. Simply extract the ZIP file, and you are ready to go.

How to do it...

To install the AWS Explore plugin in Eclipse, we need to perform the following steps:

1. Open Eclipse, and go to **Help** | **Install New Software**.
2. In the **Work with** box, type `http://aws.amazon.com/eclipse`, and press *Enter*.

3. Select **AWS Toolkit for Eclipse**, and install the plugin:

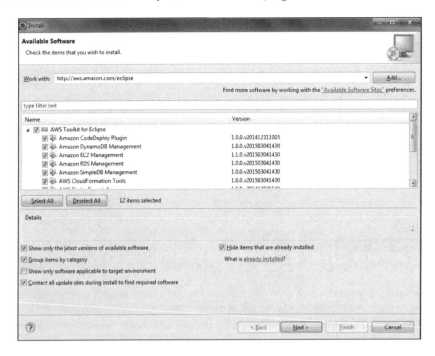

4. Once done, it will prompt you to restart Eclipse. On restart, it will give you a popup to enter your **AWS Access Key** and **Secret Key**. We have already seen how to get the AWS Access Key and Secret Key for your account. Enter this information, and you are ready to use the AWS Explorer.

5. Now, you can open the **AWS Explorer**. By selecting **Amazon DynamoDB**, you will be able to see the table that we created earlier:

6. Now, we can perform the Scan operation by specifying the conditions. For example, to get all the items of the type `book`, we can do something like this:

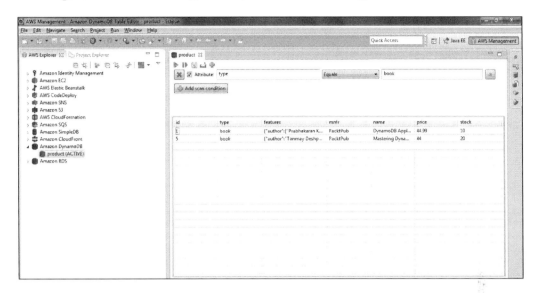

Now you can perform the various queries using this AWS Explorer.

How it works...

The AWS Explorer for Eclipse uses the Java SDK internally to make calls to DynamoDB and shows the results to us. It authenticates each call using the Access Key and Secret Key that we provided at the time of configuration.

2
Operating with DynamoDB Tables

In this chapter, we will cover the following topics:

- ▶ Creating a table using the AWS SDK for Java
- ▶ Creating a table using the AWS SDK for .Net
- ▶ Creating a table using the AWS SDK for PHP
- ▶ Updating a table using the AWS SDK for Java
- ▶ Updating a table using the AWS SDK for .Net
- ▶ Updating a table using the AWS SDK for PHP
- ▶ Listing tables using the AWS SDK for Java
- ▶ Listing tables using the AWS SDK for .Net
- ▶ Listing tables using the AWS SDK for PHP
- ▶ Deleting a table using the AWS SDK for Java
- ▶ Deleting a table using the AWS SDK for .Net
- ▶ Deleting a table using the AWS SDK for PHP

Introduction

In the previous chapter, we discussed how to perform various DynamoDB operations using the console. In this chapter, we will focus on how to use the SDK provided by Amazon to perform operations. Amazon has provided SDKs in various programming languages, out of which we are going to see operations in Java, .Net, and PHP. So, get ready to get your hands dirty with the code!

Creating a table using the AWS SDK for Java

Let's start with creating a table in DynamoDB using SDKs provided by Amazon.

Getting ready

To program various DynamoDB table operations, you can use the IDE of your choice, for example, Eclipse, NetBeans, Visual Studio, and so on. Here, we will be using the Eclipse IDE. In the previous chapter, we have already seen how to download and set up the Eclipse IDE.

How to do it...

Let's first see how to create a table in DynamoDB using the AWS SDK for Java.

You can create a **Maven** project and add the AWS SDK `Maven` dependency. The latest version available can be found at `http://mvnrepository.com/artifact/com.amazonaws/aws-java-sdk/`.

Here, I will be using Version 1.9.30, and its POM looks like this:

```
<dependency>
  <groupId>com.amazonaws</groupId>
  <artifactId>aws-java-sdk</artifactId>
  <version>1.9.30</version>
</dependency>
```

Here are the steps to create a table using the AWS SDK for Java:

1. Create an instance of the `DynamoDB` class and instantiate with the AWS `Access Key` and `Secret Key` credentials. To see the various ways on how to set credentials, you can refer to link: `http://docs.aws.amazon.com/AWSSdkDocsJava/latest/DeveloperGuide/credentials.html`:

    ```
    DynamoDB dynamoDB = new DynamoDB(new AmazonDynamoDBClient(
        new ProfileCredentialsProvider()));
    ```

2. Next, we need to create the `AttributeDefinition` and `KeySchema` elements in order to specify the keys. Here, we will create a similar table, that is, the `product` created earlier using the AWS console:

    ```
    ributeDefinition> attributeDefinitions = new ArrayLis
    finition>();
    finitions.add(new AttributeDefinition().
    buteName("id").withAttributeType("N"));
    ```

```
attributeDefinitions.add(new AttributeDefinition().
   withAttributeName("type").withAttributeType("S"));
ArrayList<KeySchemaElement> keySchema = new
   ArrayList<KeySchemaElement>();
keySchema.add(new KeySchemaElement().
   withAttributeName("id").withKeyType(KeyType.HASH));
keySchema.add(new KeySchemaElement().
   withAttributeName("type").withKeyType(KeyType.RANGE));
```

3. Now, instantiate `CreateTableRequest` by providing inputs, such as the table name, hash and range keys, and provisioned throughput. Here, we will create a table with the name `productTableJava`, and we will provide the read and write capacity units as one each:

```
CreateTableRequest request = new CreateTableRequest()
       .withTableName("productTableJava")
       .withKeySchema(keySchema)
       .withAttributeDefinitions(attributeDefinitions)
       .withProvisionedThroughput(
     new ProvisionedThroughput().withReadCapacityUnits(1L)
       .withWriteCapacityUnits(1L));
```

4. Now, invoke the `createTable` method of the `DynamoDB` class, which we instantiated earlier to actually create the table. Generally, it takes some time to see the table we created getting active, so the `waitForActive` method waits until the table is active and ready to use. Now, if we execute the method, you will see that the table has been created. You can verify this from your AWS console:

```
Table table = dynamoDB.createTable(request);
table.waitForActive();
```

5. By default, if you do not specify in which AWS region you need to create your `DynamoDB` table, it creates it in `N. Virginia`. If you need to create a table in a specific region, then you can set it at the time of the `AmazonDynamoDBClient` initiation, as follows:

```
AmazonDynamoDBClient client = new AmazonDynamoDBClient(
   new ProfileCredentialsProvider());
   client.setRegion(Region.getRegion(Regions.US_EAST_1));
DynamoDB dynamoDB = new DynamoDB(client);
```

How it works...

The AWS SDK for Java calls the API to provision the table as per the details we have provided. To authenticate the requests, AWS checks the access key and secret key that you provided at the time of API invocations.

There's more...

You can also use the `TableDescription` class to retrieve and confirm the information about the table you created:

```
TableDescription tableDescription = dynamoDB.getTable
    ("productTableJava").describe();
```

Creating a table using the AWS SDK for .Net

Now, let's understand how to create a DynamoDB table using the AWS SDK for .Net.

Getting ready

You can use an IDE, such as Visual Studio to code these recipes. You can refer to the AWS documentation on how to set up your workstation at `http://aws.amazon.com/sdk-for-net/`.

How to do it...

Let's start with creating a table called `productTableNet`:

1. Instantiate the `CreateTable` request specifying `AttributeDefinition` and `KeySchema`. We will create the table having both the HASH and RANGE Keys. We will set the provisioned read and write capacity units to be one:

   ```
   AmazonDynamoDBClient client = new AmazonDynamoDBClient();
   string tableName = "productTableNet";
   var request=new CreateTableRequest{
     AttributeDefinitions=newList<AttributeDefinition>(){
       newAttributeDefinition{
         AttributeName="id", AttributeType="N"
       },
       newAttributeDefinition{
         AttributeName="type", AttributeType="S"
       }
     },
     KeySchema=newList<KeySchemaElement>{
       newKeySchemaElement{
         AttributeName="id", KeyType="HASH"
       },
   ```

```
      newKeySchemaElement{
        AttributeName="type", KeyType="RANGE"
      }
    },
    ProvisionedThroughput=newProvisionedThroughput{
      ReadCapacityUnits=1, WriteCapacityUnits=1
    },
    TableName=tableName
};
```

2. Now, initiate the DynamoDB Client and invoke the `createTable` method to actually create the table on DynamoDB:

   ```
   var response = client.CreateTable(request);
   ```

3. Now, you can go to the DynamoDB console to confirm whether the table is created.

How it works...

Once we invoke these methods, the internal DynamoDB APIs are called to create the table with a specified feature on DynamoDB.

Creating a table using the AWS SDK for PHP

Now, let's understand how to create a DynamoDB table using the AWS SDK for PHP.

Getting ready...

You can use the IDE of your choice to code these recipes.

How to do it...

Let's start with creating a table called `productTablePHP`:

1. Instantiate the DynamoDB client for PHP. Specify the AWS region in which you wish to create the table in:

   ```
   $client = DynamoDbClient::factory(array(
       'profile' => 'default',
       'region' => 'us-west-1'
   ));
   ```

2. Invoke the `createTable` method by specifying the details, such as the table name, hash and range keys, and provisioned capacity units. Here, we will create a table with the primary key as the composite hash and range keys:

```
$result = $client->createTable(array(
    'TableName' => $tableName,
    'AttributeDefinitions' => array(
        array(
            'AttributeName' => 'id',
            'AttributeType' => 'N'
        ),
        array(
            'AttributeName' => 'type',
            'AttributeType' => 'S'
        )
    ),
    'KeySchema' => array(
        array(
            'AttributeName' => 'id',
            'KeyType' => 'HASH'
        ),
        array(
            'AttributeName' => 'name',
            'KeyType' => 'RANGE'
        )
    ),
    'ProvisionedThroughput' => array(
        'ReadCapacityUnits'  => 1,
        'WriteCapacityUnits' => 1
    )
));
```

3. Invoking this would result in the creation of a table in a specified region of AWS. You can confirm this using the AWS console.

How it works...

Once we invoke these APIs, the AWS SDK creates the table with specified details.

Updating a table using the AWS SDK for Java

Now, let's understand how to update a DynamoDB table using the AWS SDK for Java.

Getting ready...

You can use the IDE of your choice to code these recipes.

How to do it...

In this recipe, we will learn how to update the already created `DynamoDB` table. Here, we will update the read and write capacity units:

1. Create an instance of the `Table` class and initiate it by calling the `getTable` method:

   ```
   AmazonDynamoDBClient client = new AmazonDynamoDBClient(
     new ProfileCredentialsProvider());
   client.setRegion(Region.getRegion(Regions.US_EAST_1));
   DynamoDB dynamoDB = new DynamoDB(client);
   Table table = dynamoDB.getTable("productTableJava");
   ```

2. Now, create an instance of the provisioned throughput, and set the read and write capacity units. Earlier, we set the read and write capacity units to one, and now we will update it to two:

   ```
   ProvisionedThroughput provisionedThroughput =
     new ProvisionedThroughput().withReadCapacityUnits(2L).
       withWriteCapacityUnits(2L);
   ```

3. Now, invoke the `updateTable` method to see the changes in the `DynamoDB` table:

   ```
   table.updateTable(provisionedThroughput);
   ```

4. It takes time to make the changes effective, so it's good practice to wait until the table becomes active again:

   ```
   table.waitForActive();
   ```

How it works...

Once we invoke these APIs, the AWS SDK updates the table with the new changes.

Updating a table using the AWS SDK for .Net

Now, let's understand how to update a DynamoDB table using the AWS SDK for .Net.

Getting ready

You can use the IDE of your choice to code these recipes.

How to do it...

In this recipe, we will learn how to update the provisioned capacity of the already created table using the AWS SDK for .Net:

1. Create an `update table` request and provide the new read and write capacity units:

```
AmazonDynamoDBClient client = new AmazonDynamoDBClient();
string tableName = "productTableNet";
var request=new UpdateTableRequest(){
  TableName=tableName,
  ProvisionedThroughput = new ProvisionedThroughput(){
    ReadCapacityUnits=2,
      WriteCapacityUnits=2
  }
};
```

2. Invoke the `updateTable` method from the DynamoDB client to update the table with the provided capacity units:

```
var response = client.UpdateTable(request);
```

3. It takes some time for DynamoDB to make the changes effective. So, it's always a best practice to wait until the table becomes active again. By default, the AWS SDK for .Net does not provide a way to check whether the table is **ACTIVE**, so you can think about writing your own code.

How it works...

Once we invoke these APIs, the AWS SDK updates the table with the new changes.

Updating a table using the AWS SDK for PHP

Now, let's understand how to update a DynamoDB table using the AWS SDK for PHP.

Getting ready

You can use the IDE of your choice to code these recipes.

How to do it...

In this recipe, we will learn how to update the read and write capacity units for an already created table:

1. Create an instance of the DynamoDB client and invoke the `updateTable` method, providing the details of the new provisioned throughout capacity units. Here, we will update the read and write capacity units to two:

    ```
    $tableName = 'productTablePHP';
    $result = $client->updateTable(array(
        'TableName' => $tableName,
        'ProvisionedThroughput'    => array(
            'ReadCapacityUnits'    => 2,
            'WriteCapacityUnits' => 2
        )
    ));
    ```

2. DynamoDB takes some time to make the changes effective. So, it's a best practice to wait until the table gets effective again:

    ```
    $client->waitUntilTableExists(array('TableName' => $tableName));
    ```

How it works...

Once we invoke these APIs, the AWS SDK updates the table with the new changes.

Listing tables using the AWS SDK for Java

Now, let's understand how to list all the DynamoDB tables using the AWS SDK for Java.

Getting ready

You can use the IDE of your choice to code these recipes.

How to do it...

In this recipe, we will learn how to list the tables that we created earlier using the AWS SDK for Java:

1. Create an instance of the DynamoDB class and instantiate it with the AWS credential provider:

```
DynamoDB dynamoDB = new DynamoDB(new AmazonDynamoDBClient(

    new ProfileCredentialsProvider()));
```

2. Invoke the listTables method of the DynamoDB class to get a list of all the tables:

```
TableCollection<ListTablesResult> tables =
    dynamoDB.listTables();
Iterator<Table> iterator = tables.iterator();
```

3. Now, you can iterate over the list to get the details of the tables you have created:

```
while (iterator.hasNext()) {
    Table table = iterator.next();
    System.out.println(table.getTableName());
}
```

How it works...

The list table API internally calls DynamoDB services to fetch the details of the tables you have created.

Listing tables using the AWS SDK for .Net

Now, let's understand how to list all the DynamoDB tables using the AWS SDK for .Net.

Getting ready

You can use the IDE of your choice to code these recipes.

How to do it...

In this recipe, we will learn how to list the tables that we created earlier using the AWS SDK for .Net:

1. Create an instance of the DynamoDB client and invoke the `listTables` method to get all the tables that you created earlier:

```
AmazonDynamoDBClient client = new AmazonDynamoDBClient();
var response = client.ListTables();
ListTablesResult result = response.ListTablesResult;
```

2. Iterate over the `results` variable to get the names of all the tables:

```
foreach (string name in result.TableNames)
Console.WriteLine(name);
```

3. The AWS SDK for .Net also supports pagination for the list table request. If you want the list of tables to arrive in a paginated manner, then you may think of exploring it.

How it works...

The List table API internally calls DynamoDB services to fetch the details of the tables you have created.

Listing tables using the AWS SDK for PHP

Now, let's understand how to list all the DynamoDB tables using the AWS SDK for PHP.

Getting ready

You can use the IDE of your choice to code these recipes.

How to do it...

In this recipe, we will learn how to list the tables we created earlier using the AWS SDK for PHP:

1. Create an instance of the DynamoDB client and invoke the `listTables` method:

```
$client = DynamoDbClient::factory(array(
    'profile' => 'default',
    'region' => 'us-west-2'
));
$response = $client->listTables();
```

2. Iterate over the list to get the details of the tables:

```
foreach ($response['TableNames'] as $key => $value) {
        echo "$value" . PHP_EOL;
  }
```

3. The AWS SDK for PHP also provides the option to limit the number of tables that are retrieved, and it supports pagination as well. If you have a lot of tables created, then you can fetch the results in the paginated format, as follows:

```
$tablesArray = array();
do {
  $response = $client->listTables(array(
    'Limit' => 5,   // Fetching 5 tables at a time
      per page 'ExclusiveStartTableName' =>
        isset($response) ? $response
          ['LastEvaluatedTableName'] : null));

  foreach ($response['TableNames'] as $key => $value) {
    echo "$value" . PHP_EOL;
  }

  $tablesArray = array_merge($tablesArray,
    $response['TableNames']);
}
while ($response['LastEvaluatedTableName']);

// Print no. of tables

echo "Total number of tables: ";
print_r(count($tablesArray));
echo PHP_EOL;
```

How it works...

The list table API internally calls DynamoDB services to fetch the details of the tables that you have created.

Deleting a table using the AWS SDK for Java

Now, let's understand how to delete a DynamoDB table using the AWS SDK for Java.

Getting ready

You can use the IDE of your choice to code these recipes.

How to do it...

In this recipe, we will learn how to delete the table that we created earlier using the AWS SDK for Java:

1. Initialize the DynamoDB Client and call the `getTable` method by providing the name of the table that you wish to delete:

```
AmazonDynamoDBClient client = new AmazonDynamoDBClient(
   new ProfileCredentialsProvider());
client.setRegion(Region.getRegion(Regions.US_EAST_1));
DynamoDB dynamoDB = new DynamoDB(client);
Table table = dynamoDB.getTable("productTableJava");
```

2. Now, call the `delete` method of the `table` class to delete the table:

```
table.delete();
```

3. Like create and update, delete also takes some time. So, it's good practice to wait until delete takes place on DynamoDB:

```
table.waitForDelete();
```

How it works...

Once we invoke these APIs, the AWS SDK deletes the table forever. So, I request that you use this API very carefully. There is no way to get the data back once it has been deleted.

Deleting a table using the AWS SDK for .Net

Now, let's understand how to delete a DynamoDB table using the AWS SDK for .Net.

Getting ready

You can use the IDE of your choice to code these recipes.

How to do it...

In this recipe, we will learn how to delete the table that we created earlier using the AWS SDK for .Net:

1. Create a `delete` table request specifying the name of the table to be deleted:

```
string tableName = "productTableNet";
var request = new DeleteTableRequest
            {
                    TableName = tableName
            };
```

2. Invoke the `DeleteTable` method to delete the table:

```
var response = client.DeleteTable(request);
```

3. Like create and update, delete also takes some time before the changes are effective.

> **Downloading the example code**
>
> You can download the example code files from your account at http://www.packtpub.com for all the Packt Publishing books you have purchased. If you purchased this book elsewhere, you can visit http://www.packtpub.com/support and register to have the files e-mailed directly to you.

How it works...

Once we invoke these APIs, the AWS SDK deletes the table forever. So, I request that you use this API very carefully. There is no way to get the data back once it has been deleted.

Deleting a table using the AWS SDK for PHP

Now, let's understand how to delete a DynamoDB table using the AWS SDK for PHP.

Getting ready

You can use the IDE of your choice to code these recipes.

How to do it...

In this recipe, we will learn how to delete the table that we created earlier using the AWS SDK for PHP:

1. Create the `DynamoDB` Client and invoke the `deleteTable` method, specifying the name of the table to be deleted:

```
$tableName = 'productTablePHP';
$client = DynamoDbClient::factory(array(
    'profile' => 'default',
    'region' => 'us-west-2'
));
$result = $client->deleteTable(array(
    'TableName' => $tableName
));
```

2. As soon as you invoke this API, DynamoDB puts it into the DELETING status, and after a while, it has been completely deleted. It's good practice to wait until the table is deleted:

```
$client->waitUntilTableNotExists(array('TableName' =>
$tableName));
```

How it works...

Once we invoke these APIs, the AWS SDK deletes the table forever. So, I request that you use this API very carefully. There is no way to get the data back once it has been deleted.

3
Manipulating DynamoDB Items

In this chapter, we will cover the following topics:

- ▶ Putting an item into the DynamoDB table using the AWS SDK for Java
- ▶ Putting an item into the DynamoDB table using the AWS SDK for .Net
- ▶ Putting an item into the DynamoDB table using the AWS SDK for PHP
- ▶ Getting an item from the DynamoDB table using the AWS SDK for Java
- ▶ Getting an item from the DynamoDB table using the AWS SDK for .Net
- ▶ Getting an item from the DynamoDB table using the AWS SDK for PHP
- ▶ Updating an item in the DynamoDB table using the AWS SDK for Java
- ▶ Updating an item in the DynamoDB table using the AWS SDK for .Net
- ▶ Updating an item in the DynamoDB table using the AWS SDK for PHP
- ▶ Deleting an item from the DynamoDB table using the AWS SDK for Java
- ▶ Deleting an item from the DynamoDB table using the AWS SDK for .Net
- ▶ Deleting an item from the DynamoDB table using the AWS SDK for PHP
- ▶ Getting multiple items using the AWS SDK for Java
- ▶ Getting multiple items using the AWS SDK for .Net
- ▶ Getting multiple items using the AWS SDK for PHP
- ▶ Batch write operations using the AWS SDK for Java
- ▶ Batch write operations using the AWS SDK for .Net
- ▶ Batch write operations using the AWS SDK for PHP

Introduction

In the earlier chapter, we discussed how to perform various DynamoDB table operations using AWS SDKs. In this chapter, our focus is to use Amazon provided SDK to perform item operations. Amazon has provided SDKs in various programming languages, out of which we are going to see operations in Java, .NET, and PHP.

Putting an item into the DynamoDB table using the AWS SDK for Java

In the previous chapter, we saw how to create a table; now, let's see how to put items into a DynamoDB table.

Getting ready

To perform this operation, you can use the IDE of your choice. You should have also created a table in DynamoDB; if you haven't done this yet, refer to the previous chapters for details.

How to do it...

To get started, create a **maven** project, and add the AWS SDK dependency in the POM.xml. Here is the latest version of the AWS SDK for Java:

```
<dependency>
    <groupId>com.amazonaws</groupId>
    <artifactId>aws-java-sdk</artifactId>
    <version>1.9.30</version>
</dependency>
```

Once done, perform the following steps to put the items into the DynamoDB table:

1. Create an instance of the DynamoDB class and initialize it with ProfileCredentialsProvider:

   ```
   DynamoDB dynamoDB = new DynamoDB(new AmazonDynamoDBClient(
       new ProfileCredentialsProvider()));
   ```

2. Get the table in which you wish to put the item:

   ```
   Table table = dynamoDB.getTable("productTable");
   ```

3. Now, create an instance of the `item` class, and put the values into it, as follows:

```
Map<String, String> features = new HashMap<String, String>();
    features.put("camera", "13MP");
    features.put("intMem", "16GB");
    features.put("processor", "Dual-Core 1.4 GHz Cyclone
        (ARM v8-based)");
Item product = new Item()
    .withPrimaryKey(new PrimaryKey("id", 10, "type", "phone"))
    .withString("mnfr", "Samsung").withNumber("stock", 15)
    .withNumber("price", 45).withMap("features", features);
```

4. Call the `PutItem` method by passing the item created earlier, and save the details in DynamoDB:

```
PutItemOutcome outcome = table.putItem(product);
```

 If we call the `PutItem` request multiple times, and if the item with the `primary` key already exists, then the values will be updated for the same record.

How it works...

The AWS SDK for Java calls the API to put items into the table as per the details we have provided. To authenticate the requests, AWS checks the access key and secret key that you provided at the time of API invocations.

There's more...

Along with the required parameters, we can also provide optional parameters while invoking the `PutItem` method. Consider the default behavior of the `PutItem` request in which if we try to put an item with a `primary` key that already exists, the API would simply replace the item. With `ConditionExpression`, you can tell DynamoDB to update the item only if a specific condition is met; if not, it will throw `ConditionalCheckFailedException`. Now, if you wish that the `PutItem` request would replace the already existing item with the same `primary` key if a certain condition is met, you can do so.

For example, if we wish to update a product with a `primary` key as `id` 1 and type as mobile, but only if the manufacturer is Samsung, you can write the `PutItem` request like this.

```
Map<String, Object> expressionAttributeValues = new HashMap<String,
    Object>();
        expressionAttributeValues.put(":val", "Samsung");
PutItemOutcome outcome = table.putItem(product, "mnfr = :val", null,
        expressionAttributeValues);
```

Putting an item into the DynamoDB table using the AWS SDK for .Net

Let's understand how to put an item into the DynamoDB table using the AWS SDK for .Net.

Getting ready

To perform this operation, you can use the IDE of your choice.

How to do it...

Let's insert an item into DynamoDB table using the AWS SDK for .Net:

1. Create an instance of the `DynamoDB` client, and use this to put an item into the table:

```
AmazonDynamoDBClient client = new AmazonDynamoDBClient();
string tableName = "productTable";
```

2. Now, create a `PutItemRequest` with the desired parameters, and invoke the `PutItem` method:

```
var request = new PutItemRequest
{
    TableName = tableName,
    Item = new Dictionary<string, AttributeValue>()
        {
            { "id", new AttributeValue { N = "20" }},
            { "type", new AttributeValue { S = "book" }},
            { "stock", new AttributeValue { N = "110" }},
            { "price", new AttributeValue { N = "55" }},
            { "title", new AttributeValue { S = "Mastering DynamoDB"
        }},

        }
};
client.PutItem(request);
```

How it works...

The API invocations call DynamoDB services and put the item into a specified table. You can read more about the `PutItem` API at

```
http://docs.aws.amazon.com/amazondynamodb/latest/APIReference/API_
PutItem.html.
```

Putting an item into the DynamoDB table using the AWS SDK for PHP

Let's understand how to put an item into the DynamoDB table using the AWS SDK for PHP.

Getting ready

To perform this operation, you can use the IDE of your choice.

How to do it...

Let's insert item into DynamoDB table using the AWS SDK for PHP:

1. Create an instance of the DynamoDB client and initialize it with the specific AWS region and credentials:

```
$client = DynamoDbClient::factory(array(
    'profile' => 'default',
    'region' => 'us-east-1'
));
```

2. Invoke the putItem method by specifying the details of the item to be put into the DynamoDB table:

```
$response = $client->putItem(array(
    'TableName' => 'productTable',
    'Item' => array(
        'id'      => array('N'     => 30        ),
        'type'    => array('S'     => 'phone' ),
        'mnfr'    => array('S'     => 'samsung' ),
        'price'   => array('N'     => 44 ),
        'stock'   => array('N'     => 25 ),
        'name'    => array('S'     => 'Samsung Galaxy Grand 2 '
    )
    )
));
```

How it works...

The API invocations call the DynamoDB services and put the item into a specified table. You can read more about the PutItem API at http://docs.aws.amazon.com/amazondynamodb/latest/APIReference/API_PutItem.html.

Getting an item from the DynamoDB table using the AWS SDK for Java

Let's understand how to get an item from the DynamoDB table using the AWS SDK for Java.

Getting ready

To perform this operation, you can use the IDE of your choice.

How to do it...

Let's try to understand how to retrieve a stored item from the DynamoDB table using Java:

1. Create an instance of the `DynamoDB` class and initialize it with credentials:

    ```
    AmazonDynamoDBClient client = new AmazonDynamoDBClient(
        new ProfileCredentialsProvider());
    client.setRegion(Region.getRegion(Regions.US_EAST_1));
    DynamoDB dynamoDB = new DynamoDB(client);
    ```

2. Get the `table` by specifying the name:

    ```
    Table table = dynamoDB.getTable("productTable");
    ```

3. Invoke the `GetItem` request by specifying the `primary` key of the item:

    ```
    Item product = table.getItem(new PrimaryKey("id", 10, "type",
    "phone"));
    ```

    Here, we have a table with the composite hash and range keys, so we have to provide values for both keys.

How it works...

The API invocations call the `DynamoDB` services and get the item from a specified table. You can read more about the `PutItem` API at http://docs.aws.amazon.com/amazondynamodb/latest/APIReference/API_PutItem.html.

Getting an item from the DynamoDB table using the AWS SDK for .Net

Let's understand how to get an item from the DynamoDB table using the AWS SDK for .Net.

Getting ready

To perform this operation, you can use the IDE of your choice.

How to do it...

Let's try to understand how to retrieve a stored item from the DynamoDB table using .Net:

1. Create an instance of the `DynamoDB` client:

```
AmazonDynamoDBClient client = new AmazonDynamoDBClient();
string tableName = "productTable";
```

2. Create a `GetItemRequest` that specifies the `primary` key details:

```
var request = new GetItemRequest
  {
     TableName = tableName,
     Key = new Dictionary<string,AttributeValue>() {
         {"id",new AttributeValue{ N="20"}
     },
     {"type", new AttributeValue{ S="phone"}
     }
  },
  };
```

Here, we have a composite primary key as the ID and type.

3. Invoke the `GetItem` method with a specified request, and fetch the items from the results:

```
var response = client.GetItem(request);
var result = response.GetItemResult;
```

How it works...

The API invocations call the DynamoDB services and get the item from a specified table.

Getting an item from the DynamoDB table using the AWS SDK for PHP

Let's understand how to get an item from the DynamoDB table using the AWS SDK for PHP.

Getting ready

To perform this operation, you can use the IDE of your choice.

How to do it...

Let's try to understand how to retrieve a stored item from the DynamoDB table using PHP:

1. Create an instance of the `DynamoDB` client and initialize it with the AWS region and credentials:

```
$client = DynamoDbClient::factory(array(
    'profile' => 'default',
    'region' => 'us-east-1'
));
```

2. Call the `getItem` method by specifying the `primary` key used for the table:

```
$response = $client->getItem(array(
    'TableName' => 'productTable',
    'Key' => array(
        'id' => array( 'N' => 30 ),
        'type' => array( 'S' => 'phone' )
    )
));
```

3. You can `print` the response if required:

```
print_r ($response['Item']);
```

How it works...

The API invocations call the DynamoDB services and get the item from the specified table.

Updating an item in the DynamoDB table using the AWS SDK for Java

Let's understand how to update an item from the DynamoDB table using the AWS SDK for Java.

Getting ready

To perform this operation, you can use the IDE of your choice.

How to do it...

Let's try to understand how to update a stored item in the DynamoDB table using Java. The `update` request allows us to add a new attribute to the item, update the value of an attribute, or remove an attribute from the item:

1. Create an instance of the `DynamoDB` class and initialize it with credentials:

```
AmazonDynamoDBClient client = new AmazonDynamoDBClient(
    new ProfileCredentialsProvider());
client.setRegion(Region.getRegion(Regions.US_EAST_1));
DynamoDB dynamoDB = new DynamoDB(client);
```

2. Get the `table` by specifying the name:

```
Table table = dynamoDB.getTable("productTable");
```

3. Create a map of `ExpressionAttributeValues` in which you need to specify the attributes that you wish to update:

```
Map<String, String> expressionAttributeNames = new HashMap<String,
String>();
        expressionAttributeNames.put("#R", "rating");
        expressionAttributeNames.put("#S", "stock");
        expressionAttributeNames.put("#M", "mnfr");
Map<String, Object> expressionAttributeValues = new
HashMap<String,
    Object>();
        expressionAttributeValues.put(":val1", 5);
        expressionAttributeValues.put(":val2", 2);
```

   Here, I want to add an attribute called `rating` with the value as 5, update/reduce the value of `stock` by 2, and remove the `mnfr` attribute from that item.

4. The last thing that I need to do is call the `updateItem` method by specifying the earlier mentioned actions. We also need to provide the `primary` key for which item you wish to see these changes. Here, in our case, we are using the composite hash and range keys, so we will have to mention both of them:

```
UpdateItemOutcome outcome = table.updateItem("id", 10, "type",
"phone", "ADD #R :val1 SET #S = #S - :val2 REMOVE #M",
    expressionAttributeNames, expressionAttributeValues);
```

Here, we need to follow certain conventions, which are as follows

▸ Attribute names should start with #

▸ Attribute values should start with a colon (:)

▸ Multiple actions should be separated by a comma (,)

How it works...

The API invocations call the DynamoDB services and update the item from a specified table.

There's more...

You can also use `ConditionalExpression` in order to do conditional updates. For example, if you are planning to update the stock of a certain product, and you want to make sure that the update should only happen if the current value of that attribute is what you are expecting it to be. The following snippet explains how to implement `ConditionalExpression` while updating an item:

```
Table table = dynamoDB.getTable("productTable");
Map<String, String> expressionAttributeNames = new HashMap<String,
String>();
        expressionAttributeNames.put("#S", "stock");
Map<String, Object> expressionAttributeValues = new HashMap<String,
Object>();
        expressionAttributeValues.put(":val1", 50);   // update Stock
to 50
        expressionAttributeValues.put(":val2", 20);   // only if
existing stock is 20
UpdateItemOutcome outcome = table.updateItem(
        new PrimaryKey("id",10, "type","phone"),
        "SET #S = :val1", // UpdateExpression
        "#S = :val2",      // ConditionalExpression
        expressionAttributeNames,
            expressionAttributeValues);
```

Updating an item in the DynamoDB table using the AWS SDK for .Net

Let's understand how to update an item from the DynamoDB table using the AWS SDK for .Net.

Getting ready

To perform this operation, you can use the IDE of your choice.

How to do it...

Let's try to understand how to update a stored item in the DynamoDB table using .Net. The update request allows us to add a new attribute to the item, update the value of an attribute, or remove an attribute from the item:

1. Create an instance of the `DynamoDB` client:

```
AmazonDynamoDBClient client = new AmazonDynamoDBClient();
string tableName = "productTable";
```

2. Create the `update` table request and specify the details of the attributes that you wish to update. Here, I want to add an attribute called `rating` with the value as `5`, update/reduce the value of `stock` by 2, and remove the `mnfr` attribute from that item, whose `primary` key `id` is `10` and the type `phone`:

```
var request = new UpdateItemRequest
{
    TableName = tableName,
    Key = new Dictionary<string,AttributeValue>() { { "id", new
        AttributeValue { N = "20" } },
    { "type", new AttributeValue { S = "phone" }},
    ExpressionAttributeNames = new Dictionary<string,string>()
    {
        {"#R", "rating"},
        {"#S", "stock"},
        {"#M", "mnfr"}
    },
    ExpressionAttributeValues = new Dictionary<string,
AttributeValue>()
    {
        {":val1",new AttributeValue { N = "5"}},
        {":val2",new AttributeValue {N = "2"}}
    },
    UpdateExpression = "ADD #R :val1 SET #S = #S - :val2 REMOVE
#M"
};
```

3. Now, call the `updateItem` method to invoke the request:

```
var response = client.UpdateItem(request);
```

How it works...

The API invocations call the DynamoDB services and update the item from a specified table.

There's more...

You can also use `ConditionalExpression` in order to do conditional updates. For example, if you are planning to update the stock of a certain product, and you want to make sure that the update should only happen if the current value of that attribute is what you are expecting it to be. The following snippet explains how to implement `ConditionalExpression` while updating an item:

```
var request = new UpdateItemRequest
{
    Key = new Dictionary<string,AttributeValue>() { { "id",
        new AttributeValue { N = "10" } }, { "type", new
AttributeValue
            { S = "phone" } }     },
                ExpressionAttributeNames = new
Dictionary<string,string>()
        {
            {"#S", "stock"}
        },
    ExpressionAttributeValues = new Dictionary<string,
AttributeValue>()
        {
            {":newprice",new AttributeValue {N = "50"}},
            // Update stock to 50 only if
            {":currprice",new AttributeValue {N = "20"}} // Current value
is 20
        },
    UpdateExpression = "SET #S = :newprice",
    ConditionExpression = "#S = :currprice",
    TableName = tableName,
    ReturnValues = "ALL_NEW"
};
```

Updating an item in the DynamoDB table using the AWS SDK for PHP

Let's understand how to update an item from the DynamoDB table using the AWS SDK for PHP.

Getting ready

To perform this operation, you can use the IDE of your choice.

How to do it...

Let's try to understand how to update a stored item in the DynamoDB table using PHP. The `update` request allows us to add a new attribute to the item, update the values of an attribute, or remove an attribute from the item:

1. Create an instance of the `DynamoDBClient` and initialize it with the desired AWS region and credentials:

```
$client = DynamoDbClient::factory(array(
    'profile' => 'default',
    'region' => 'us-east-1'
));
```

2. Create the `Update` item request and specify the details. Here, I want to add an attribute called `rating` with the value as 5, update/reduce the value of `stock` by 2, and remove the `mnfr` attribute from that item whose `primary` key `id` is 10 and the type `phone`:

```
$response = $client->updateItem(array(
    'TableName' => 'productTable',
        'Key' => array(
            'id' => array('N' => 10), 'type' => array( 'S' =>
'phone' )
            ),
        'ExpressionAttributeValues' =>  array (
            ':val1' => array('N' => '5'),
            ':val2' => array('N' => '2')
        ) ,
        'UpdateExpression' => 'SET rating = :val1, stock = stock -
:val2
            REMOVE mnfr'
));
```

3. You may `print` the response to see the outcome:

```
print_r($response);
```

How it works...

The API invocations call the DynamoDB services and update the item from a specified table.

There's more...

You can also use `ConditionalExpression` in order to do conditional updates. For example, if you are planning to update the stock of a certain product, and you want to make sure that the update should happen only if the current value of that attribute is what you are expecting it to be. The following snippet explains how to implement `ConditionalExpression` while updating an item:

```
$response = $client->updateItem(array(
    'TableName' => 'productTable',
    'Key' => array(
        'id' => array('N' => 10), 'type' => array( 'S' => 'phone' )
    ),
    'ExpressionAttributeValues' =>  array (
        ':val1' => array('N' => 50),
        ':val2' => array('N' => 20)
    ) ,
    'UpdateExpression' => 'SET stock = :val1',
    'ConditionExpression' => 'stock = :val2',
    'ReturnValues' => 'ALL_NEW'
));
```

Deleting an item from the DynamoDB table using the AWS SDK for Java

Let's understand how to delete an item from the DynamoDB table using the AWS SDK for Java.

Getting ready

To perform this operation, you can use the IDE of your choice.

How to do it...

Let's try to understand how to delete a stored item from the DynamoDB table using Java:

1. Create an instance of the DynamoDB class and initialize it with the desired AWS region and credentials:

    ```
    AmazonDynamoDBClient client = new AmazonDynamoDBClient(
        new ProfileCredentialsProvider());
    client.setRegion(Region.getRegion(Regions.US_EAST_1));
    DynamoDB dynamoDB = new DynamoDB(client);
    ```

2. Get the table from which you wish to delete the item:

    ```
    Table table = dynamoDB.getTable("productTable");
    ```

3. Invoke the deleteItem method from the Table class by specifying the item's primary key. Here, in our case, we are using the composite hash and range keys, so we will have to mention both of them:

    ```
    DeleteItemOutcome outcome = table.deleteItem(new PrimaryKey("id",
    10, "type", "phone"));
    ```

How it works...

The API invocations call the DynamoDB services and delete the item from a specified table. Once the data is deleted, there is no way to get it back. So, I would request that you use this with care.

There's more...

You can also use ConditionalExpression to do conditional deletes. With this feature, you can first check the value of a certain attribute in DynamoDB, and then it should be deleted. For example, if you want to delete an item only if it's discontinued, then you can write something like this:

```
Table table = dynamoDB.getTable("productTable");
Map<String, Object> expressionAttributeValues = new HashMap<String,
Object>();
expressionAttributeValues.put(":val", true);
DeleteItemOutcome outcome = table.deleteItem("id", 10, "type",
"mobile",
    "isDiscontinued = :val", null, expressionAttributeValues);
```

Deleting an item from the DynamoDB table using the AWS SDK for .Net

Let's understand how to delete an item from the DynamoDB table using the AWS SDK for .Net.

Getting ready

To perform this operation, you can use the IDE of your choice.

How to do it...

Let's try to understand how to delete a stored item from the DynamoDB table using .Net:

1. Create an instance of the `DynamoDBClient` class:

```
AmazonDynamoDBClient client = new AmazonDynamoDBClient();
string tableName = "productTable";
```

2. Create a `delete` table request and specify the key of the item that you wish to delete from the table. Here, we will specify both the `hash` and `range` keys, as we have created a table with the composite `primary` keys:

```
var request = new DeleteItemRequest
{
    TableName = tableName,
    Key = new Dictionary<string,AttributeValue>()
{
{ "id", new AttributeValue { N = "20" } },
    { "type", new AttributeValue { S = "phone" }}
}
};
```

3. Invoke the `DeleteItem` method specifying the request:

```
var response = client.DeleteItem(request);
```

How it works...

The API invocations call the DynamoDB services and delete the item from the specified table. Once the data has been deleted, there is no way to get it back. So, I would request that you use this with care.

There's more...

You can also use `ConditionalExpression` to do conditional deletes. With this feature, you can first check the value of a certain attribute in DynamoDB, and then it should be deleted. For example, if you want to delete an item only if it's discontinued, then you can write something like this:

```
var request = new DeleteItemRequest
{
    TableName = tableName,
    Key = new Dictionary<string,AttributeValue>() { { "id", new At
    tributeValue { N = "201" } }, { "type", new AttributeValue { S =
        "phone" } }},
     ReturnValues = "ALL_OLD",
    ExpressionAttributeNames = new Dictionary<string, string>()
    {
        {"#ISD", "isDiscontinued"}
    },
    ExpressionAttributeValues = new Dictionary<string,
AttributeValue>()
    {
        {":val",new AttributeValue {BOOL = true}}
    },
    ConditionExpression = "#ISD = :val"
};
var response = client.DeleteItem(request);
```

Deleting an item from the DynamoDB table using the AWS SDK for PHP

Let's understand how to delete an item from the DynamoDB table using the AWS SDK for PHP.

Getting ready

To perform this operation, you can use the IDE of your choice.

How to do it...

Let's try to understand how to delete a stored item from the DynamoDB table using PHP:

1. Create an instance of the DynamoDB client and initiate it with the desired AWS region and credentials:

```
$client = DynamoDbClient::factory(array(
    'profile' => 'default',
    'region' => 'us-east-1'
));
```

2. Invoke the `deleteItem` method specifying the primary key of the item to be deleted:

```
$response = $client->deleteItem(array(
    'TableName' => 'productTable',
    'Key' => array(
        'id' => array(
            'N' => 30
        ),
    'type' => array(
            'S' => 'phone'
        )
    )
));
```

How it works...

The API invocations call the DynamoDB services and delete the item from the specified table. Once the data has been deleted, there is no way to get it back. So, I would request that you use this with care.

There's more...

You can also use `ConditionalExpression` to do conditional deletes. With this feature, you can first check the value of a certain attribute in `DynamoDB`, and then it should be deleted. For example, if you want to delete an item only if it's discontinued, then you can write something like this:

```
$tableName = "productTablePHP";
$response = $client->deleteItem ( array (
    'TableName' => $tableName,
    'Key' => array(
        'id' => array(
```

```
            'N' => 30
        ),
        'type' => array(
            'S' => 'phone'
        )
    ),
    'ExpressionAttributeValues' => array(
        ':val1' => array('BOOL' => true)
    ),
    'ConditionExpression' => 'isDiscontinued = :val1',
    'ReturnValues' => 'ALL_OLD'
) );
```

Getting multiple items using the AWS SDK for Java

Let's understand how to get multiple items from the DynamoDB table using the AWS SDK for Java.

Getting ready

To perform this operation, you can use the IDE of your choice.

How to do it

Let's try to understand how to get multiple stored items from the DynamoDB table using Java:

1. Create an instance of the `DynamoDB` class and initialize it with the desired AWS region and credentials:

   ```
   AmazonDynamoDBClient client = new AmazonDynamoDBClient(
       new ProfileCredentialsProvider());
   client.setRegion(Region.getRegion(Regions.US_EAST_1));
   DynamoDB dynamoDB = new DynamoDB(client);
   ```

2. Create an instance of the `TableKeyAndAttributes` class, and add the `primary` key details of the items you wish to retrieve using in one go:

   ```
   TableKeysAndAttributes productKeysAndAttributes = new TableKeysAnd
   Attributes("productTable");
   productKeysAndAttributes.addHashAndRangePrimaryKey("id", 10,
   "type",
       "phone");
   ```

```
productKeysAndAttributes.addHashAndRangePrimaryKey("id", 20,
"type",
    "phone");
```

Now, we can simply call the `batchGetItem` method to get the required items:

```
BatchGetItemOutcome outcome = dynamoDB .batchGetItem
    (productKeysAndAttributes);

for (String tableName : outcome.getTableItems().keySet()) {
    System.out.println("Items in table " + tableName);
    List<Item> items = outcome.getTableItems().get(tableName);
        for (Item item : items) {
            System.out.println(item);
        }
    }
}
```

How it works...

The `BatchGetItem` can be used to get items from one or more tables. At a time, an operation can return up to 16 MB of data, which can be up to 100 items. If the data limit or provisioned throughput exceeds any of the table, or if any internal failure occurs, the API will return partial results. If the API returns the partial results, then the operation returns a value of `UnprocessedKeys`. We can use this value to retry the operation, starting with the next item to fetch.

By default, the `BatchGetItem` operation performs consistent reads. If you need consistent reads, then you can mention that for any table or all the tables.

Note that the `BatchGetItem` operation is performed in parallel, so this operation does not get give any guarantee of the order of the item retrieval. So, while designing your application, it's good to include primary key of attributes in `ProjectionAttributes` so that it becomes easy for us to decide the order.

Getting multiple items using the AWS SDK for .Net

Let's understand how to get multiple items from the DynamoDB table using the AWS SDK for .Net.

Getting ready

To perform this operation, you can use the IDE of your choice.

How to do it...

Let's try to understand how to get multiple stored items from the DynamoDB table using .Net:

1. Create an instance of the `AmazonDynamoDBClient` class:

```
AmazonDynamoDBClient client = new AmazonDynamoDBClient();
string tableName = "productTable";
```

2. Create `BatchGetItemRequest` specifying the items to be fetched. You can also fetch multiple items together from various tables:

```
var request = new BatchGetItemRequest
{
  RequestItems = new Dictionary<string, KeysAndAttributes>()
  {
    {
      tableName,
      new KeysAndAttributes
      {
        Keys = new List<Dictionary<string, AttributeValue>>()
        {
          new Dictionary<string, AttributeValue>()
          {
            { "id", new AttributeValue { N = 10 } },
            { "type", new AttributeValue { S = "phone" } }
          },
          new Dictionary<string, AttributeValue>()
          {
            { "id", new AttributeValue { N = 20 } },
            { "type", new AttributeValue { S = "phone" } }
          }
        }
      }
    }
  }
};
```

3. Now, we can invoke `batchGetItem` specifying the request that we created earlier:

```
var response = client.BatchGetItem(request);
```

How it works...

The `BatchGetItem` operation can be used to get items from one or more tables. At a time, an operation can return up to 16 MB of data, which can be up to 100 items. If the data limit or provisioned throughput exceeds any of the table, or if any internal failure occurs, then the API will return partial results. If the API returns the partial results, then the operation returns a value of `UnprocessedKeys`. We can use this value to retry the operation starting with the next item to fetch.

By default, the `BatchGetItem` operation performs consistent reads. If you need consistent reads, then you can mention that for any table or all the tables.

Note that the `BatchGetItem` operation is performed in parallel, so this operation does not get give any guarantee of the order of the item retrieval. So, while designing your application, it's good to include the primary keys of attributes in `ProjectionAttributes` so that it becomes easy for us to decide the order.

Getting multiple items using the AWS SDK for PHP

Let's understand how to get multiple items from the DynamoDB table using the AWS SDK for PHP.

Getting ready...

To perform this operation, you can use the IDE of your choice.

How to do it...

Let's try to understand how to get multiple stored items from the DynamoDB table using PHP:

1. Create an instance of the `DynamoDB` client and initialize it with the desired AWS region and credentials:

   ```
   $client = DynamoDbClient::factory(array(
       'profile' => 'default',
       'region' => 'us-east-1'
   ));
   ```

2. Create the `batchGetItem` request and provide the `primary` keys of items to be fetched:

   ```
   $response = $client->batchGetItem(array(
   ```

```
        "RequestItems" => array(
            "Reply" => array(
                "Keys" => array(
                    array(
                        "id"   => array( 'N' => "10"),
                        "type" => array( 'S' => "phone"),
                    ),
                    array(
                        "id"   => array( 'S' => "20"),
                        "type" => array( 'S' => "phone"),
                    ),
                )
            )
        )
    ));
```

How it works...

The BatchGetItem operation can be used to get items from one or more tables. At a time, an operation can return up to 16 MB of data, which can be up to 100 items. If the data limit or provisioned throughput exceeds any of the table, or if any internal failure occurs, then the API will return partial results. If the API returns the partial results, then the operation returns a value of UnprocessedKeys. We can use this value to retry the operation starting with the next item to fetch.

By default, the BatchGetItem operation eventually performs consistent reads. If you need consistent reads, then you can mention that for any table or all the tables.

Note that the BatchGetItem operation is performed in parallel, so this operation does not get give guarantee of the order of the item retrieval. So, while designing your application, it's good to include the primary keys of attributes in ProjectionAttributes so that it becomes easy for us to decide the order.

Batch write operations using the AWS SDK for Java

Let's understand how to put or delete multiple items from the DynamoDB table using the AWS SDK for Java.

Getting ready

To perform this operation, you can use the IDE of your choice.

How to do it...

Let's try to understand how to put/delete items from the DynamoDB table using Java:

1. Create an instance of the `DynamoDB` class and initialize it with the desired AWS region and credentials:

   ```
   AmazonDynamoDBClient client = new AmazonDynamoDBClient(
       new ProfileCredentialsProvider());
       client.setRegion(Region.getRegion(Regions.US_EAST_1));
   DynamoDB dynamoDB = new DynamoDB(client);
   ```

2. Create instance of `TableWriteItems` and specify if you wish to put or delete items from the DynamoDB table:

   ```
   TableWriteItems productItems = new TableWriteItems("productTable")
       .withItemsToPut(
           new Item().withPrimaryKey("id", 40, "type", "book")
               .withString("title", "DynamoDB Cookbook"))
           .withPrimaryKeysToDelete(
               new PrimaryKey("id", 10, "type", "phone"));
   ```

3. Now, invoke the `batchWriteItem` method to see the changes:

   ```
   BatchWriteItemOutcome outcome = dynamoDB.
   batchWriteItem(productItems);
   ```

How it works...

The `BatchWriteItem` operation can be used to put or delete multiple items from various tables in a single call. The `BatchWriteItem` operation can put/delete 25 items, which is up to 16 MB of data in an operation. The `BatchWriteItem` operation is rejected if one or more tables do not exist, if the request contains more than 25 items, if any of the item is more than 400 KB, or if the total data size exceeds 16 MB.

Once the data has been deleted, there is no way to get it back.

Batch write operations using the AWS SDK for .Net

Let's understand how to put or delete multiple items from the DynamoDB table using the AWS SDK for .Net.

Getting ready

To perform this operation, you can use the IDE of your choice.

How to do it...

Let's try to understand how to put/delete items from the DynamoDB table using .Net.

1. Create an instance of the `AmazonDynamoDBClient` class:

```
AmazonDynamoDBClient client = new AmazonDynamoDBClient();
string tableName = "productTable";
```

2. Create the `BatchWriteItem` request instance and specify the items that you wish to put or delete:

```
var request = new BatchWriteItemRequest
  {
    RequestItems = new Dictionary<string, List<WriteRequest>>
      {
        {
          tableName, new List<WriteRequest>
          {
            new WriteRequest
            {
              PutRequest = new PutRequest
              {
                Item = new Dictionary<string,AttributeValue>
                {
                  { "id", new AttributeValue { N = 40 } },
                  { "type", new AttributeValue { S = "book" } },
                  { "title", new AttributeValue { S = "DynamoDB
                      Cookbook" } }
                }
              }
            },
            new WriteRequest
            {
              DeleteRequest = new DeleteRequest
              {
                Key = new Dictionary<string,AttributeValue>()
                {
```

```
                    { "id", new AttributeValue { N = 10 } },
                    { "type", new AttributeValue { S = "phone" } }
                }
            }
        }
    }
};
```

3. Invoke the `BatchGetItem` method specifying the request to see the changes:

```
response = client.BatchWriteItem(request);
```

How it works...

The `BatchWriteItem` operation can be used to put or delete multiple items from various tables in a single call. The `BatchWriteItem` operation can put/delete 25 items, which is up to 16 MB of data in an operation. The `BatchWriteItem` operation is rejected if one more tables do not exist, if the request contains more than 25 items request, if any of the item is more than 400 KB, or if the total data size exceeds 16 MB.

Once the data has been deleted, there is no way to get it back.

Batch write operations using the AWS SDK for PHP

Let's understand how to put or delete multiple items from the DynamoDB table using the AWS SDK for PHP.

Getting ready

To perform this operation, you can use the IDE of your choice.

How to do it...

Let's try to understand how to put/delete items from the DynamoDB table using PHP:

1. Create an instance of the `DynamoDB` client and initialize it with the desired AWS region and credentials:

```
$client = DynamoDbClient::factory(array(
    'profile' => 'default',
    'region' => 'us-east-1'
));
```

2. Create an instance of the `batchWriteItem` request by specifying which items you wish to put or delete from the DynamoDB table:

```
$response = $client->batchWriteItem(array(
    "RequestItems" => array(
        $tableName => array(
            array(
                "PutRequest" => array(
                    "Item" => array(
                        "id"    => array('N' => 40),
                        "type" => array('S' => "book"),
                        "title"=> array('S' => "DynamoDB
Cookbook")
                    ))
            ),
            array(
                "DeleteRequest" => array(
                    "Key" => array(
                        "id"    => array('N' => 10),
                        "type" => array('S' => "phone"),
                    ))
            )
        )
    )
));
```

How it works...

The `BatchWriteItem` can be used to put or delete multiple items from various tables in a single call. The `BatchWriteItem` operation can put/delete 25 items, which is up to 16 MB of data in an operation. The `BatchWriteItem` operation is rejected if one more tables do not exist, or if the request contains more than 25 items request, or if any of the item is more than 400 KB, or if the total data size exceeds 16 MB.

Once the data is deleted, there is no way to get it back.

4
Managing DynamoDB Indexes

In this chapter, we will cover the following topics:

- ▶ Creating a DynamoDB table with a Global Secondary Index using the AWS SDK for Java

- ▶ Creating a DynamoDB table with a Global Secondary Index using the AWS SDK for .Net

- ▶ Creating a DynamoDB table with a Global Secondary Index using the AWS SDK for PHP

- ▶ Querying a Global Secondary Index using the AWS SDK for Java

- ▶ Querying a Global Secondary Index using the AWS SDK for .Net

- ▶ Querying a Global Secondary Index using the AWS SDK for PHP

- ▶ Creating a DynamoDB table with a Local Secondary Index using the AWS SDK for Java

- ▶ Creating a DynamoDB table with a Local Secondary Index using the AWS SDK for .Net

- ▶ Creating a DynamoDB table with a Local Secondary Index using the AWS SDK for PHP

- ▶ Querying a Local Secondary Index using the AWS SDK for Java

- ▶ Querying a Local Secondary Index using the AWS SDK for .Net

- ▶ Querying a Local Secondary Index using the AWS SDK for PHP

- ▶ Using a Global Secondary Index for quick lookups

Introduction

DynamoDB enables faster access to the data using indexes. We saw how to fetch items using primary key indexes in the previous chapter. Sometimes, accessing data only through primary keys is just not enough. In order to avail data access through non-primary key attributes, we need to create secondary indexes. When we create a secondary index, DynamoDB copies the projected attributes along with the key attributes. The secondary index allows you to scan or query the way we do it for a table. There are two types of secondary indexes that we can create on the DynamoDB table: a **Global Secondary Index** (**GSI**) and a **Local Secondary Index** (**LSI**).

A GSI allows you to query data on the complete table dataset, as it has completely different hash and range keys compared to a LSI. A LSI restricts you to querying data on only one partition as it has the same hash key as that of the table, so the query is local for a given hash key. A LSI needs to be created at the time of the table creation itself, while a GSI can be added to an existing table at any point in time. A GSI supports only consistent queries, while a LSI allows you to choose between strong or eventual consistent queries. By default, a LSI executes a query of a consistent nature.

In the earlier chapters, we discussed how to perform various DynamoDB item operations using AWS SDKs. In this chapter, we will focus on how to use the SDK provided by Amazon to perform secondary index-related operations. Amazon has provided SDKs in various programming languages, out of which here we are going to see operations in Java, .Net, and PHP.

Creating a DynamoDB table with a Global Secondary Index using the AWS SDK for Java

In the earlier chapters, we have seen how to create a table; now, let's see how to create a DynamoDB table with a Global Secondary Index.

Getting ready

To perform this recipe, you can use the IDE of your choice.

How to do it...

To get started, create a **maven** project, and add the AWS SDK dependency to the POM.xml file. Here is the latest version of the AWS SDK for Java:

```
<dependency>
  <groupId>com.amazonaws</groupId>
```

```
<artifactId>aws-java-sdk</artifactId>
<version>1.9.34</version>
</dependency>
```

Once done, perform the following steps to create a DynamoDB table with a Global Secondary Index:

1. Create an instance of the DynamoDB class and initialize it with `ProfileCredentialsProvider`:

    ```
    AmazonDynamoDBClient client = new AmazonDynamoDBClient(
        new ProfileCredentialsProvider());
        client.setRegion(Region.getRegion(Regions.US_EAST_1));
    DynamoDB dynamoDB = new DynamoDB(client);
    ```

2. Create the attribute definitions that we created earlier for the table creation recipe. Here, we will create the table named `productTable` with the primary key attributes as `id` and `type`:

    ```
    ArrayList<AttributeDefinition> attributeDefinitions = new
        ArrayList<AttributeDefinition>();
        attributeDefinitions.add(new
            AttributeDefinition().withAttributeName(
                "id").withAttributeType("N"));
        attributeDefinitions.add(new
            AttributeDefinition().withAttributeName(
                "type").withAttributeType("S"));
        attributeDefinitions.add(new
            AttributeDefinition().withAttributeName("name")
                .withAttributeType("S"));
        attributeDefinitions.add(new AttributeDefinition()
            .withAttributeName("mnfr").withAttributeType("S"));
    ArrayList<KeySchemaElement> keySchema = new
        ArrayList<KeySchemaElement>();
    keySchema.add(new KeySchemaElement()
        .withAttributeName("id")
        .withKeyType(KeyType.HASH));
    keySchema.add(new KeySchemaElement()
        .withAttributeName("type")
        .withKeyType(KeyType.RANGE));
    ```

3. Now, create an instance of the Global Secondary Index, providing a meaningful name and provisioned throughput with read and write capacity units. We also need to mention the attributes we need to project in this index. In this example, we select the `ALL` attributes:

    ```
    GlobalSecondaryIndex nameMnfrIndex = new GlobalSecondaryIndex()
        .withIndexName("NameManufacturer")
    ```

```
        .withProvisionedThroughput(
            new ProvisionedThroughput().withReadCapacityUnits(
                (long) 10).withWriteCapacityUnits((long) 1))
        .withProjection( new Projection()
        .withProjectionType(ProjectionType.ALL));
```

4. Once done, we need to create the key schema and set it to the index we created. We use the name as the HASH Key and mnfr (manufacturer) as the RANGE Key attribute for this index:

```
ArrayList<KeySchemaElement> indexKeySchema = new
    ArrayList<KeySchemaElement>();
indexKeySchema.add(new KeySchemaElement()
    .withAttributeName("name")
    .withKeyType(KeyType.HASH));
indexKeySchema.add(new KeySchemaElement().
withAttributeName("mnfr")
    .withKeyType(KeyType.RANGE));
nameMnfrIndex.setKeySchema(indexKeySchema);
```

5. Now, it's time to initialize the createTableRequest function, and add the CreateTable method to invoke the DynamoDB class:

```
CreateTableRequest request = new CreateTableRequest()
    .withTableName("productTable")
    .withKeySchema(keySchema)
    .withAttributeDefinitions(attributeDefinitions)
    .withGlobalSecondaryIndexes(nameMnfrIndex)
    .withProvisionedThroughput(new ProvisionedThroughput()
    .withReadCapacityUnits(1L)
            .withWriteCapacityUnits(1L));
Table table = dynamoDB.createTable(request);
```

How it works...

The AWS SDK for Java calls the API to create the table as per the details we have provided, along with the secondary index we mentioned. To authenticate the requests, AWS checks the access key and secret key you provided at the time of API invocations.

One thing to note here is that if we are planning to use certain attributes as keys of a secondary index, then we need to provide their definitions at the time of defining the table key attributes. Make sure that you wait before you perform any other operation, as DynamoDB takes some time to create the table and makes it active before it can be used. Nowadays, AWS allows you to add GSIs to an existing table as well.

Creating a DynamoDB table with a Global Secondary Index using the AWS SDK for .Net

Now, let's see how to create a DynamoDB table with a Global Secondary Index using the AWS SDK for .Net.

Getting ready

To perform this recipe, you can use the IDE of your choice.

How to do it...

In the earlier chapters, we have seen how to create a DynamoDB table. Now, we are going to see how to create a DynamoDB table using a Global Secondary Index:

1. Create `AttributesDefinitions` and the key schema. Make sure that you specify the attributes you are going to use as hash and range keys in the Global Secondary Index:

```
AttributeDefinitions = new List<AttributeDefinition>(){
    new AttributeDefinition{
        AttributeName="id", AttributeType="N"
    },
    new AttributeDefinition{
        AttributeName="type", AttributeType="S"
    },
    new AttributeDefinition{
        AttributeName="name", AttributeType="S"
    },
    new AttributeDefinition{
        AttributeName="mnfr", AttributeType="S"
    }
    };
    // Table key schema
    var tableKeySchema = new List<KeySchemaElement>()
    {
        new KeySchemaElement{AttributeName="id", KeyType="HASH"
    },
    new KeySchemaElement{ AttributeName="type", KeyType="RANGE"
    }
};
```

2. Create a `GlobalSecondaryIndex`, and specify the provisioned throughput read and write capacity units. You should also specify the hash and range key attributes for this index:

```
var nameMnfrIndex = new GlobalSecondaryIndex
{
    IndexName = "NameManfrIndex",
    ProvisionedThroughput = new ProvisionedThroughput
    {
        ReadCapacityUnits = (long)5,
        WriteCapacityUnits = (long)5
    },
    Projection = new Projection { ProjectionType = "ALL" }
};

var indexKeySchema = new List<KeySchemaElement> {
    {new KeySchemaElement { AttributeName = "name",
        KeyType = "HASH"}},
    {new KeySchemaElement{AttributeName = "mnfr",KeyType =
"RANGE"}}
};
nameMnfrIndex.KeySchema = indexKeySchema;
```

3. Now invoke `CreateTableRequest` to specify the provisioned throughput of the table, and set the Global Secondary Index we created earlier:

```
string tableName = "productTable";
CreateTableRequest createTableRequest = new CreateTableRequest
{
    TableName = tableName,
    ProvisionedThroughput = new ProvisionedThroughput
    {
        ReadCapacityUnits = (long)5,
        WriteCapacityUnits = (long)5
    },
    AttributeDefinitions = attributeDefinitions,
    KeySchema = tableKeySchema,
    GlobalSecondaryIndexes = { nameMnfrIndex }
};
```

4. Now simply invoke the `createTable` method by providing the request we created, and you will see that the table is created with the Global Secondary Index:

```
CreateTableResponse response =
    client.CreateTable(createTableRequest);
```

How it works...

Refer to the *How it works...* section from the, *Creating a DynamoDB table with a Global Secondary Index using the AWS SDK for Java* recipe.

Creating a DynamoDB table with a Global Secondary Index using the AWS SDK for PHP

Now let's see how to create a DynamoDB table with a Global Secondary Index using the AWS SDK for PHP.

Getting ready

To perform this recipe, you can use the IDE of your choice.

How to do it...

In the earlier chapters, we have seen how to create a DynamoDB table. Now, we are going to see how to create a DynamoDB table using a Global Secondary Index:

1. Instantiate the `DynamoDB` client for PHP. Specify the AWS region in which you wish to create the table:

```
$client = DynamoDbClient::factory(array(
    'profile' => 'default',
    'region' => 'us-west-1'
));
```

2. Now we have to initialize the create table request, specifying the `AttributesDefinition`, `KeySchema`, and `GlobalSecondaryIndex` specifications. Here, we will use `id` and `type` as the table hash and range keys, respectively, while `name` and `mnfr` will be used as the hash and range keys for the global secondary index:

```
$tableName = "productTable";
$result = $client->createTable(array(
    'TableName' => $tableName,
    'AttributeDefinitions' => array(
        array(
            'AttributeName' => 'id',
            'AttributeType' => 'N'
        ),
```

```
            array(
                'AttributeName' => 'type',
                'AttributeType' => 'S'
            ),
            array(
                'AttributeName' => 'name',
                'AttributeType' => 'S'
            ),array(
                'AttributeName' => 'mnfr',
                'AttributeType' => 'S'
            )
        ),
        'KeySchema' => array(
            array(
                'AttributeName' => 'id',
                'KeyType' => 'HASH'
            ),
            array(
                'AttributeName' => 'type',
                'KeyType' => 'RANGE'
            )
        ),
        'GlobalSecondaryIndexes' => array(
            array(
                'IndexName' => 'NameManufacturerIndex',
                'ProvisionedThroughput' => array (
                    'ReadCapacityUnits' => 5,
                    'WriteCapacityUnits' => 5
                ),
                'KeySchema' => array(
                    array(
                        'AttributeName' => 'name',
                        'KeyType' => 'HASH'
                    ),
                    array(
                        'AttributeName' => 'mnfr',
                        'KeyType' => 'RANGE'
                    )
                ),
                'Projection' => array(
                    'ProjectionType' => 'ALL'
                )
```

```
            )
        ),
        'ProvisionedThroughput' => array(
            'ReadCapacityUnits'     => 5,
            'WriteCapacityUnits' => 5
        )
    ));
```

3. This will create the table with the global secondary index.

How it works...

Refer to the *How it works...* section from the recipe, *Creating a DynamoDB table with a Global Secondary Index using the AWS SDK for Java*.

Querying a Global Secondary Index using the AWS SDK for Java

Now, we are going to see how to query a global secondary index. This will help us fetch the required items as per the query conditions.

Getting ready

To perform this recipe, you can use the IDE of your choice. To perform a query operation, you should first add items using the AWS Console or SDK, as we have seen in the earlier chapters.

How to do it...

The Query API on a Global Secondary Index is similar to the Query API on a DynamoDB table. Perform the following operations in order to query the index:

1. Create an instance of the `DynamoDB` class and initialize it with the credentials. Also, get the table from DynamoDB on which you wish to perform the query operation:

```
AmazonDynamoDBClient client = new AmazonDynamoDBClient(
    new ProfileCredentialsProvider());
client.setRegion(Region.getRegion(Regions.US_EAST_1));
DynamoDB dynamoDB = new DynamoDB(client);
Table product = dynamoDB.getTable("product");
```

2. Get the `Index` to be queried on:

```
Index nameMnfrIndex = product.getIndex("NameManufacturer");
```

3. Now, specify the query specifications, and invoke the `query` method to get the results. Here, we want to fetch the items whose `name` is `S3`. For this, we need to write the following code in the given manner:

```
QuerySpec spec = new QuerySpec().withHashKey("name", "S3");
ItemCollection<QueryOutcome> items = nameMnfrIndex.query(spec);
for (Item item : items) {
System.out.println(item.toJSONPretty());
}
```

4. In a similar manner, you can specify the other conditions to fetch the items.

How it works...

The Query API works similarly to the way in which it works for table query operations. As we mentioned earlier, DynamoDB copies the data to the secondary indexes and creates the hash and range indexing on that copied data. When we query for this index, all the requests are routed to the secondary index itself.

Querying a Global Secondary Index using the AWS SDK for .Net

Now, we are going to see how to query a Global Secondary Index.

Getting ready

To perform this operation, you can use the IDE of your choice. To perform a query operation, you should first add items using the AWS Console or SDK, as we have seen in the earlier chapters.

How to do it...

The Query API on the Global Secondary Index is similar to the Query API on a DynamoDB table. Perform the following operations in order to query the index:

1. Initiate the DynamoDB client with the credentials:

```
client = new AmazonDynamoDBClient();
```

2. Create an instance of `QueryRequest`, specifying the keys of items you wish to fetch from the secondary index. Here, we want to fetch the item whose hash key name is `S3`:

```
QueryRequest queryRequest = new QueryRequest
{
    TableName = "product",
```

```
        IndexName = "NameManfrIndex",
        KeyConditionExpression = "#nm = :v_name",
        ExpressionAttributeNames = new Dictionary<String,
            String> {
            {"#nm", "name"}
        },
        ExpressionAttributeValues = new Dictionary< string,
            AttributeValue> {
            {":v_name", new AttributeValue { S =  "S3" }}
        }
        };
```

3. Now, execute the Query method to get the results:

```
var result = client.Query(queryRequest);
```

How it works...

Refer to the *How it works...* section from the recipe, *Querying a Global Secondary Index using the AWS SDK for Java*.

Querying a Global Secondary Index using the AWS SDK for PHP

Now, we are going to see how to query a global secondary index using the AWS SDK for PHP.

Getting ready

To perform this operation, you can use the IDE of your choice. To perform a query operation, you should first add items using the AWS Console or SDK, as we have seen in the earlier chapters.

How to do it...

The Query API on a Global Secondary Index is similar to the query API on a DynamoDB table. Perform the following operations in order to query the index:

1. Instantiate the `DynamoDB` client for PHP. Specify the AWS region in which you wish to create the table:

```
$client = DynamoDbClient::factory(array(
    'profile' => 'default',
    'region' => 'us-west-1'
));
```

2. Invoke the query method from the DynamoDB client by specifying the secondary index keys on which you wish to perform the query. Here, we want to fetch all the products whose name is S3:

```
$tableName = 'product';

$response = $client->query(array(
    'TableName' => $tableName,
    'IndexName' => 'NameManufacturerIndex',
    'KeyConditionExpression' => '#nm = :v_name',
    'ExpressionAttributeNames' => array (
        '#nm' => 'name'),
    'ExpressionAttributeValues' =>  array (
        ':v_name' => array('S' => 'S3')
    ),
    'Select' => 'ALL_ATTRIBUTES'
));
```

3. Lastly, we can parse the response to get the desired attribute values.

How it works...

Refer to the *How it works...* section from the recipe, *Querying a Global Secondary Index using the AWS SDK for Java*.

Creating a DynamoDB table with a Local Secondary Index using the AWS SDK for Java

As mentioned earlier, we have seen how to create a table with a global secondary index; now, let's see how to create a table with a local secondary index.

Getting ready

To perform this operation, you can use the IDE of your choice.

How to do it...

To get started, create a **maven** project, and add the AWS SDK dependency to the `POM.xml`. Here is the latest version of the AWS SDK for Java:

1. Create an instance of the `DynamoDB` class and initialize it with `ProfileCredentialsProvider`:

```
AmazonDynamoDBClient client = new AmazonDynamoDBClient(
    new ProfileCredentialsProvider());
        client.setRegion(Region.getRegion(Regions.US_EAST_1));
DynamoDB dynamoDB = new DynamoDB(client);
```

2. Create the attribute `definitions` we created earlier for the table creation recipe. Here, we will create the table named `productTable` with the primary key attributes as `id` and `type`:

```
ArrayList<AttributeDefinition> attributeDefinitions =
    new ArrayList<AttributeDefinition>();
attributeDefinitions.add(new AttributeDefinition()
    .withAttributeName("id").withAttributeType("N"));
attributeDefinitions.add(new AttributeDefinition()
    .withAttributeName("type").withAttributeType("S"));
attributeDefinitions.add(new AttributeDefinition()
    .withAttributeName("mnfr").withAttributeType("S"));
ArrayList<KeySchemaElement> keySchema = new
    ArrayList<KeySchemaElement>();
keySchema.add(new KeySchemaElement().withAttributeName("id")
    .withKeyType(KeyType.HASH));
keySchema.add(new KeySchemaElement().withAttributeName("type")
    .withKeyType(KeyType.RANGE));
```

3. Create an instance of the local secondary index and provide the attributes to be projected:

```
LocalSecondaryIndex idMnfrIndex = new LocalSecondaryIndex()
    .withIndexName("IdManufacturerIndex").withProjection(
        new Projection()
            .withProjectionType(ProjectionType.ALL));
```

4. Now create an `indexkeyschema`, specifying the same hash key as the table hash key and range key, as the alternate attributes on which you wish to create the local secondary index:

```
ArrayList<KeySchemaElement> indexKeySchema = new
    ArrayList<KeySchemaElement>();
```

```
indexKeySchema.add(new KeySchemaElement()
    .withAttributeName("id")
    .withKeyType(KeyType.HASH));
indexKeySchema.add(new KeySchemaElement()
    .withAttributeName("mnfr")
        .withKeyType(KeyType.RANGE));
idMnfrIndex.setKeySchema(indexKeySchema);
```

5. Now initiate the create table request, specifying the table and index key schema. We also need to specify the provisioned throughput:

```
CreateTableRequest request = new CreateTableRequest()
    .withTableName("productTable")
    .withKeySchema(keySchema)
    .withAttributeDefinitions(attributeDefinitions)
    .withLocalSecondaryIndexes(idMnfrIndex)
    .withProvisionedThroughput(new ProvisionedThroughput()
        .withReadCapacityUnits(1L)
            .withWriteCapacityUnits(1L));
```

6. Now create the invoke `createtable` method with the aforementioned request to see that the table gets created:

```
Table table = dynamoDB.createTable(request);
```

How it works...

A LSI needs to be created at the time of table creation itself. A LSI gives you the option to have a choice of range keys. Unlike a GSI, in a LSI we need to use the same hash key as the table hash key. AWS puts size constraints per distinct hash key value. We are allowed to store up to 10 GB of data per distinct hash key value. This number includes all the items in the table plus all the items in the indexes, so we have to make sure that the size limitations are considered while creating a LSI.

Creating a DynamoDB table with a Local Secondary Index using the AWS SDK for .Net

Now, let's see how to create a DynamoDB table with a Local Secondary Index using the AWS SDK for .Net.

Getting ready

To perform this operation, you can use the IDE of your choice.

How to do it...

In the earlier chapters, we have seen how to create a DynamoDB table. Now we are going to see how to create a DynamoDB table using a Local Secondary Index:

1. Create `AttributesDefinitions` and the key schema. Make sure that you specify the attributes you are going to use as the hash and range keys in the Global Secondary Index:

```
AttributeDefinitions = new List<AttributeDefinition>(){
    new AttributeDefinition{
        AttributeName="id",
        AttributeType="N"
    },
    new AttributeDefinition{
        AttributeName="type",
        AttributeType="S"
    },
    new AttributeDefinition{
        AttributeName="mnfr",
        AttributeType="S"
    }
};
// Table key schema
var tableKeySchema = new List<KeySchemaElement>()
{
    new KeySchemaElement{
        AttributeName="id",
        KeyType="HASH"
    },
    new KeySchemaElement{
        AttributeName="type",
        KeyType="RANGE"
    }
};
```

2. Create an `indexkeyschema` specifying the same hash key as the table hash key, while specifying the attribute as an index range key on which you wish to query the table:

```
List<KeySchemaElement> indexKeySchema = new
List<KeySchemaElement>();
indexKeySchema.Add(new KeySchemaElement() { AttributeName =
    "id", KeyType = "HASH" });
```

```
indexKeySchema.Add(new KeySchemaElement() { AttributeName =
    "mnfr", KeyType = "RANGE" });
Projection projection = new Projection() { ProjectionType =
    "INCLUDE" };
```

Here, we mention the `Projectiontype` to be `INCLUDE`, which means that only the specified table attributes are projected to the index.

3. Now, create a Local Secondary Index specifying the meaningful name and the index key schema:

```
LocalSecondaryIndex localSecondaryIndex = new
LocalSecondaryIndex()
{
    IndexName = "IdManufacturerIndex",
    KeySchema = indexKeySchema,
    Projection = projection
};


List<LocalSecondaryIndex> localSecondaryIndexes = new
List<LocalSecondaryIndex>();
localSecondaryIndexes.Add(localSecondaryIndex);
```

4. Now, invoke `CreateTableRequest` to specify the provisioned throughput of the table, and set the Global Secondary Index we created earlier:

```
CreateTableRequest createTableRequest = new CreateTableRequest
{
    TableName = tableName,
    ProvisionedThroughput = new ProvisionedThroughput
    {
        ReadCapacityUnits = (long)5,
        WriteCapacityUnits = (long)5
    },
    AttributeDefinitions = attributeDefinitions,
    KeySchema = tableKeySchema,
LocalSecondaryIndexes = { localSecondaryIndexes }
};
```

5. Now, simply invoke the `createTable` method by providing the request we created, and you will see that the table is created with a Global Secondary Index:

```
CreateTableResponse response =
    client.CreateTable(createTableRequest);
```

How it works...

Refer to the *How it works...* section from the recipe, *Creating a DynamoDB table with a Local Secondary Index using the AWS SDK for Java*.

Creating a DynamoDB table with a Local Secondary Index using the AWS SDK for PHP

Now, let's see how to create a DynamoDB table with a Local Secondary Index using the AWS SDK for PHP.

Getting ready

To perform this operation, you can use the IDE of your choice.

How to do it...

In the earlier chapters, we have seen how to create a DynamoDB table. Now we are going to see how to create a DynamoDB table using a Local Secondary Index:

1. Instantiate the `DynamoDB` client for PHP. Specify the AWS region in which you would wish to create the table:

```
$client = DynamoDbClient::factory(array(
    'profile' => 'default',
    'region' => 'us-west-1'
));
```

2. Now, we have to initialize the `createtable` request specifying the `AttributesDefinition`, `KeySchema`, and `LocalSecondaryIndex` specifications. Here, we will use `id` and `type` as the table hash and range keys, respectively, while `id` and `mnfr` will be used as hash and range keys for the local secondary index:

```
$result = $client->createTable(array(
    'TableName' => $tableName,
    'AttributeDefinitions' => array(
        array(
            'AttributeName' => 'id',
            'AttributeType' => 'N'
        ),
```

```
                array(
                    'AttributeName' => 'type',
                    'AttributeType' => 'S'
                ),array(
                    'AttributeName' => 'mnfr',
                    'AttributeType' => 'S'
                )
            ),
            'KeySchema' => array(
                array(
                    'AttributeName' => 'id',
                    'KeyType' => 'HASH'
                ),
                array(
                    'AttributeName' => 'type',
                    'KeyType' => 'RANGE'
                )
            ), 'LocalSecondaryIndexes' => array(
                array(
                    'IndexName' => 'IdManufacturerIndex',
                    'KeySchema' => array(
                        array(
                            'AttributeName' => 'id',
                            'KeyType' => 'HASH'
                        ),
                        array(
                            'AttributeName' => 'mnfr',
                            'KeyType' => 'RANGE'
                        )
                    ),
                    'Projection' => array(
                        'ProjectionType' => 'INCLUDE'
                    )
                )
            ),   ),
            'ProvisionedThroughput' => array(
                'ReadCapacityUnits'  => 5,
                'WriteCapacityUnits' => 5
            )
        ));
```

3. This will create the table with the Local Secondary Index.

How it works...

Refer to the *How it works...* section from the *Creating a DynamoDB table with a Local Secondary Index using the AWS SDK for Java* recipe.

Querying a Local Secondary Index using the AWS SDK for Java

Now, we are going to see how to query a local secondary index.

Getting ready

To perform this operation, you can use the IDE of your choice. To perform a query operation, you should first add items using the AWS Console or SDK, as we have seen in the earlier chapters.

How to do it...

The Query API on a Local Secondary Index is similar to the query API on a DynamoDB table. Perform the following operations in order to query the index:

1. Create an instance of the DynamoDB class and initialize it with the credentials. Also, get the table from DynamoDB on which you wish to perform the query operation:

```
AmazonDynamoDBClient client = new AmazonDynamoDBClient(
    new ProfileCredentialsProvider());
client.setRegion(Region.getRegion(Regions.US_EAST_1));
DynamoDB dynamoDB = new DynamoDB(client);
Table product = dynamoDB.getTable("product");
```

2. Get the index to be queried on:

```
Index idMnfrIndex = product.getIndex("IdManufacturerIndex");
```

3. Now specify the query specifications, and invoke the query method to get the results. Here, we want to fetch the items whose id is 1 and mnfr is samsung. For this, we need to write the following code in the given manner:

```
QuerySpec spec = new QuerySpec().withKeyConditionExpression(
    "id = :v_id AND mnfr = :v_mnfr").withValueMap(
        new ValueMap().withNumber(":v_id", 1).withString(
            ":v_mnfr", "samsung"));
ItemCollection<QueryOutcome> items = index.query(spec);
Iterator<Item> itemsIter = items.iterator();
Iterator<Item> itemsIter = items.iterator();
```

```
while (itemsIter.hasNext()) {
    Item item = itemsIter.next();
    System.out.println(item.toJSONPretty());
}
```

4. In a similar manner, you can specify the other conditions to fetch the items.

How it works...

The Query API works in exactly the same way that it works for table query operations. Like the table range keys, DynamoDB stores the LSI in a sorted manner. When queried, DynamoDB looks for the exact hash key specified in the request, and then narrows down the search by comparing the index key conditions.

Note that the `KeyConditionExpression` specification is part of the AWS SDK 1.9.34, so make sure that you have the right version with you.

Querying a Local Secondary Index using the AWS SDK for .Net

Now, we are going to see how to query a local secondary index.

Getting ready

To perform this operation, you can use the IDE of your choice. To perform the query operation, you should first add items using the AWS Console or SDK, as we have seen in the earlier chapters.

How to do it...

The Query API on a Local Secondary Index is similar to the query API on a DynamoDB table. Perform the following operations in order to query the index:

1. Initiate the `DynamoDB` client with the credentials:

   ```
   client = new AmazonDynamoDBClient();
   ```

2. Create an instance of `QueryRequest` specifying the keys of items you wish to fetch from the secondary index. Here, we want to fetch the item whose hash key is `1` and `mnfr` is `samsung`. We also need to mention to return `ALL_ATTRIBUTES` present in the resulted item:

   ```
   QueryRequest queryRequest = new QueryRequest
   {
       TableName = "product",
   ```

```
    IndexName = "IdManufacturerIndex",
    Select = "ALL_ATTRIBUTES",
    ScanIndexForward = true,
    KeyConditionExpression = "id = :v_id AND mnfr = :v_mnfr",
        ExpressionAttributeValues = new Dictionary<string,
            AttributeValue>()
    {
        {":v_id",new AttributeValue {N = "1"}},
        {":v_mnfr",new AttributeValue {S = "samsung"}}
    },
};
```

3. Now execute the `Query` method to get the results:

```
var result = client.Query(queryRequest);
```

How it works...

Refer to the *How it works...* section from the *Querying a Local Secondary Index using the AWS SDK for Java* recipe.

Querying a Local Secondary Index using the AWS SDK for PHP

Now we are going to see how to query a Local secondary index using the AWS SDK for PHP.

Getting ready

To perform this operation, you can use the IDE of your choice. To perform the query operation, you should first add items using the AWS Console or SDK, as we have seen in the earlier chapters.

How to do it...

The Query API on a Local Secondary Index is similar to the query API on a DynamoDB table. Perform the following operations in order to query the index:

1. Instantiate the `DynamoDB` client for PHP. Specify the AWS region in which you would wish to create the table:

```
$client = DynamoDbClient::factory(array(
    'profile' => 'default',
    'region' => 'us-west-1'
));
```

2. Invoke the `query` method from the `DynamoDB` client, specifying the local index keys on which you wish to perform the query. Here, we want to fetch all the products whose `id` is 1 and `mnfr` is `samsung`:

```
$tableName = 'product';
$response = $client->query(array(
    'TableName' => $tableName,
    'IndexName' => 'IdManufacturerIndex',
    'KeyConditionExpression' => 'id = :v_id AND mnfr >= :v_mnfr',
    'ExpressionAttributeValues' =>  array (
        ':v_id' => array('N' => '1'),
        ':v_mnfr' => array('S' => 'samsung')
    ),
    'Select' => 'ALL_ATTRIBUTES'
));
```

3. Lastly, we can parse the response to get the desired attribute values.

How it works...

Refer to the *How it works...* section from the recipe, *Querying a Local Secondary Index using the AWS SDK for Java*.

Using a Global Secondary Index for quick lookups

Sometimes, we may want to do a quick lookup on attributes, which are not part of the DynamoDB table keys; in that case, we can create a Global Secondary Index, specifying the required attributes as the index keys.

Getting ready

We will perform this operation using the table we created earlier.

How to do it...

Consider the e-commerce application we have been following up in this book, where we have a product table whose hash and range keys are the `id` and `type` of the product. Now, consider a use case where you want to have an updated view of the product price and stock. In that case, you can create a GSI on the attribute called the product name, and you will project only the stock and price of the product in the GSI.

We can create the table with a GSI, as we saw in the earlier recipes, with a slight modification. Earlier, we had projected all the attributes; now we can project only the required attributes, such as the stock and price. A sample projection definition is shown as follows:

```
Projection projection = new Projection()
.withProjectionType(ProjectionType.INCLUDE);
ArrayList<String> nonKeyAttributes = new ArrayList<String>();
nonKeyAttributes.add("stock");
nonKeyAttributes.add("price");
projection.setNonKeyAttributes(nonKeyAttributes);
GlobalSecondaryIndex nameIndex = new GlobalSecondaryIndex()
    .withIndexName("Name")
    .withProvisionedThroughput(
        new ProvisionedThroughput().withReadCapacityUnits(
            (long) 10).withWriteCapacityUnits((long) 1))
            .withProjection(projection);
ArrayList<KeySchemaElement> indexKeySchema = new
    ArrayList<KeySchemaElement>();
indexKeySchema.add(new KeySchemaElement()
    .withAttributeName("name")
    .withKeyType(KeyType.HASH));
nameIndex.setKeySchema(indexKeySchema);
```

How it works...

When we create a GSI with only specific projected attributes, DynamoDB only returns those attributes on the query, along with the key attributes. It will not return any other attributes.

5
Exploring Higher Level Programming Interfaces for DynamoDB

In this chapter, we will cover the following topics:

- ▸ Creating a data model for the DynamoDB item using the object persistence model in Java
- ▸ Putting items into the DynamoDB table using the object persistence model in Java
- ▸ Retrieving items from the DynamoDB table using the object persistence model in Java
- ▸ Creating a custom object for the DynamoDB table using the object persistence model in Java
- ▸ Querying items from the DynamoDB table using the object persistence model in Java
- ▸ Scanning items from the DynamoDB table using the object persistence model in Java
- ▸ Saving items into the DynamoDB table using the object persistence model in .Net
- ▸ Retrieving items from the DynamoDB table using the object persistence model in .Net
- ▸ Creating a custom object for the DynamoDB table using the object persistence model in .Net
- ▸ Querying items from the DynamoDB table using the object persistence model in .Net
- ▸ Scanning items from the DynamoDB table using the object persistence model in .Net

Introduction

In the previous chapter, we discussed how to use secondary indexes to improve data access in DynamoDB. In this chapter, we will discuss how to use the object persistence model to perform various operations in DynamoDB. DynamoDB provides APIs for the object persistence model as an out-of-the-box feature of its SDKs. These APIs only support item-level operations; they don't support table or secondary indexes level operations, so to perform recipes given in this chapter, you need to have at least a table created using any of the methods described in the earlier chapters.

The object persistence model helps you create and maintain applications in a much cleaner and neater way. The annotation-based implementation provides great readability and is easy to use.

Creating a data model for the DynamoDB item using the object persistence model in Java

To start with, we first need to create a data model. In this recipe, we will see how to create the item data model that is saved in a particular table.

Getting ready

To perform this recipe, you should already have a table created with you. We have already seen how to create a table in DynamoDB using various methods, such as the console, SDKs, and so on. To perform this operation, you can use the IDE of your choice.

How to do it...

Let's create a data model for DynamoDB:

1. To get started, we need to create a **maven** project and add the AWS SDK dependency to the pom.xml. Here is the latest version of the AWS SDK for Java:

    ```
    <dependency>
      <groupId>com.amazonaws</groupId>
      <artifactId>aws-java-sdk</artifactId>
      <version>1.9.34</version>
    </dependency>
    ```

2. Once done, complete the following to set up the DynamoDB model. We are going to use the same example that we have been using since the first chapter. Here, we will create the `object` class for the `Product` table. We can use DynamoDB annotations to specify the table name, hash key, range key, and so on. Here is a sample `object` class:

```
@DynamoDBTable(tableName = "ProductOPM")
public class Product {

  private int id;
  private int type;
  private String title;
  private String mnfr;
  private Map<String, String> features;
  @DynamoDBHashKey(attributeName = "id")
  public int getId() {
    return id;
  }
  public void setId(int id) {
  this.id = id;
  }
  @DynamoDBRangeKey(attributeName = "type")
  public int getType() {
    return type;
  }
  public void setType(int type) {
    this.type = type;
  }
  @DynamoDBAttribute(attributeName = "title")
  public String getTitle() {
    return title;
  }
  public void setTitle(String title) {
    this.title = title;
  }
  @DynamoDBAttribute(attributeName = "mnfr")
  public String getMnfr() {
    return mnfr;
  }
  public void setMnfr(String mnfr) {
    this.mnfr = mnfr;
```

```
    }
    @DynamoDBAttribute(attributeName = "features")
    public Map<String, String> getFeatures() {
      return features;
    }
    public void setFeatures(Map<String, String> features) {
      this.features = features;
    }
  }
```

There are also various other annotations available, such as @DynamoDBAutoGeneratedKey, @DynamoDBDocument, @DynamoDBIndexHashKey, and @DynamoDBIndexRangeKey. You can read more about the various other annotations at http://docs.aws.amazon.com/amazondynamodb/latest/developerguide/JavaDeclarativeTagsList.html.

How it works...

The AWS SDK provides various sets of annotations that are used for the object persistence model. As we annotate the attribute, it will perform the role in the DynamoDB table. If you wish for the DynamoDB API to ignore an attribute from its processing, then you can annotate this attribute like @DynamoDBIgnore.

Putting items into the DynamoDB table using the object persistence model in Java

Now, we are going to see how to put items into the table using the object persistence model.

Getting ready

Before we start this recipe, the object model needs to be created in the previous recipe.

How to do it...

Let's see how to put items into the table using the object persistence model:

1. Create an instance of the DynamoDB client class, and initiate it with the credential's profile. You can also set the region if you have created the table in a specific region:

```
AmazonDynamoDBClient client = new AmazonDynamoDBClient(
    new ProfileCredentialsProvider());
  client.setRegion(Region.getRegion(Regions.US_EAST_1));
```

2. Create an instance of the `DynamoDBMapper` class, and initiate it with the client that we created earlier:

```
DynamoDBMapper mapper = new DynamoDBMapper(client);
```

3. Create an instance of the `Product` class, which we created in the earlier recipe, and set the desired values in the objects:

```
Product product = new Product();
  product.setId(10);
  product.setType("book");
  product.setTitle("DynamoDB Cookbook");
  product.setMnfr("PacktPub");
  Map<String, String> features = new HashMap<String,
    String>();
  features.put("camera", "13MP");
  product.setFeatures(features);
```

4. Lastly, call the `save()` method of the mapper by passing the value of the product and the object in order to save the data in the DynamoDB table:

```
mapper.save(product);
```

How it works...

The AWS SDK internally calls the HTTP APIs to perform operations. The object persistence model's APIs help us perform various operations in a cleaner way. We can also call the batch write APIs to put the items in bulk. To save multiple items in one go, we can create the objects and call the `batchSave()` method, as shown in the following code:

```
mapper.batchSave(Array.asList(product1, product2, product3));
```

Retrieving items from the DynamoDB table using the object persistence model in Java

Now, we are going to see how to get items from the table using the object persistence model.

Getting ready

To perform this recipe, you should have set up the project, as described in the earlier recipes, specifically, `pom.xml`, dependencies, and the object model.

How to do it...

Let's use the object persistence model to retrieve the items:

1. Create an instance of the `DynamoDB client` class and initiate it with the credential's profile. You can also set the region if you have created the table in a specific region:

```
AmazonDynamoDBClient client = new AmazonDynamoDBClient(
    new ProfileCredentialsProvider());
    client.setRegion(Region.getRegion(Regions.US_EAST_1));
```

2. Create an instance of the `DynamoDBMapper` class and initiate it with the client that we created earlier:

```
DynamoDBMapper mapper = new DynamoDBMapper(client);
```

3. Now, invoke the `load` method, specifying the keys of the item that you wish to retrieve, and it will fetch the records:

```
Product retrievedProduct = mapper.load(Product.class, 10, "book");
```

Here, we are giving both the hash and range keys of the items that we wish to retrieve.

How it works...

The AWS SDK internally calls the HTTP APIs to perform the operations. One thing that we need to ensure is that if we have a table that has the composite hash and range keys, it's mandatory to provide both of them while using the load method.

Creating a custom object for the DynamoDB table using the object persistence model in Java

Now, we are going to see how to create a custom object as an attribute while using the object persistence model.

Getting ready

To perform this recipe, you should have set up the project, as described in the earlier recipes, specifically `pom.xml`, and also set up dependencies and the object model.

How to do it...

Sometimes, we need custom composite objects in order to represent our data models. Suppose that in our product table, we want to store the dimensions of the product; to do so, we can create the class of this type and use the `DynamoDBMarshalling` annotation. While doing so, we also need to specify the converter in which we have to specify to read and write data.

Let's create a custom object for DynamoDB table:

1. Create the `custom` class by providing the attributes and getter setter method:

```
public class Dimension {
  private int length;
  private int width;
  private int height;
  public int getLength() {
    return length;
  }
  public void setLength(int length) {
    this.length = length;
  }
  public int getWidth() {
    return width;
  }
  public void setWidth(int width) {
    this.width = width;
  }
  public int getHeight() {
    return height;
  }
  public void setHeight(int height) {
    this. height = height;
  }
}
```

2. Next, we need to create an object of this class as an attribute in the `Product` class. Here, we have to annotate it with `@DynamoDBMarshalling`. We also need to provide the `converter` class in which we have to override the two methods: the `marshall` method that will convert the object values into a string and the `unmarshall` method that will read the string in order to put it into the object again. Here is a sample `converter` class:

```
public class DimensionsConverter implements
DynamoDBMarshaller<Dimension> {
```

```
public String marshall(Dimension dimension) {
  String dimStr = String.format("%sx %s x %s", dimension.
getLength(),
    dimension.getHeight(), dimension.getWidth());
    return dimStr;
  }
public Dimension unmarshall(Class<Dimension> dimension, String
value) {
    String[] dimValues = value.split("x");
    Dimension dimension = new Dimension();
  dimension.setLength(Integer.parseInt
    (dimValues[0].trim()));
  dimension.setHeight(Integer.parseInt
    (dimValues[1].trim()));
  dimension.setWidth(Integer.parseInt
    (dimValues[2].trim()));
  return dimension;
  }
}
```

3. Now, we can use this implementation to save and retrieve the data, which is similar to the previous recipes.

How it works...

Marshalling and unmarshalling helps us deal with complex data more easily and naturally. The `marshall` and `unmarshall` methods get invoked depending on whether you are reading the data from DynamoDB or writing to it.

Querying items from the DynamoDB table using the object persistence model in Java

Now, we are going to see how to query items from the table using the object persistence model.

Getting ready

To perform this recipe, you should have set up the project, as described in the earlier recipes, specifically, `pom.xml`, dependencies, and the object model.

How to do it...

Let's query items from the table using the object persistence model:

1. Create an instance of the DynamoDB client class and initiate it with the credential's profile. You can also set the region if you have created the table in a specific region:

```
AmazonDynamoDBClient client = new AmazonDynamoDBClient(
    new ProfileCredentialsProvider());
  client.setRegion(Region.getRegion(Regions.US_EAST_1));
```

2. Create an instance of the DynamoDBMapper class and initiate it with the client that we created earlier:

```
DynamoDBMapper mapper = new DynamoDBMapper(client);
```

3. To query the item, we first need to create query expressions and key conditions, as shown in the following code. Here, we want to fetch all the items whose id is 10 and type starts with the character b:

```
// Hash key condition - id =10
   Product prodHashKeyValue = new Product();
   prodHashKeyValue.setId(10);
// Range key condition - type whose values starts with b
   Condition rangeKeyCondition = new Condition().
withComparisonOperator(
     ComparisonOperator.BEGINS_WITH.toString())
     .withAttributeValueList(new
       AttributeValue().withS("b"));
// Write query expression
DynamoDBQueryExpression<Product> queryExpression = new
  DynamoDBQueryExpression<Product>()
     .withHashKeyValues(prodHashKeyValue)
       .withRangeKeyCondition("type", rangeKeyCondition);
```

4. Now, invoke the query method to get the items that meet the specified conditions:

```
PaginatedQueryList<Product> queriedProducts = mapper.query(
    Product.class, queryExpression);
  for (Product product : queriedProducts) {
    System.out.println(product.toString());
  }
```

Exploring Higher Level Programming Interfaces for DynamoDB

How it works...

The AWS SDK internally calls the HTTP APIs to perform the operations. Here, while performing range key conditions, we can use various conditional operators, such as equal to, greater than equal to, less than equal to, begins with, between, and so on, provided they meet the data type criteria.

Scanning items from the DynamoDB table using the object persistence model in Java

Now, we are going to see how to scan items from the table using the object persistence model.

Getting ready

To perform this recipe, you should have set up the project, as described in the earlier recipes, specifically, pom.xml, dependencies, and the object model.

How to do it...

Let's scan items from the table using the object persistence model:

1. Create an instance of the DynamoDB client class and initiate it with the credential's profile. You can also set the region if you have created the table in a specific region:

    ```
    AmazonDynamoDBClient client = new AmazonDynamoDBClient(
        new ProfileCredentialsProvider());
        client.setRegion(Region.getRegion(Regions.US_EAST_1));
    ```

2. Create an instance of the DynamoDBMapper class and initiate it with the client that we created earlier:

    ```
    DynamoDBMapper mapper = new DynamoDBMapper(client);
    ```

3. Scanning allows us to put filter conditions. Here, suppose that we want to get all the items whose type is book; in this case, we can use a scan operation. To do so, we need to create a scan filter expression and condition, as follows:

    ```
    // Condition type equal to book
    Condition condition = new Condition().withComparisonOperator(
        ComparisonOperator.EQ.toString()).withAttributeValueList(
        new AttributeValue().withS("book"));
    ```

108

```
DynamoDBScanExpression scanExpression = new
DynamoDBScanExpression();
scanExpression.addFilterCondition("type", condition);
```

4. Now, invoke the `scan` method of the mapper to get the scan results:

```
PaginatedScanList<Product> products = mapper.scan(Product.class,
scanExpression);
for (Product product : products) {
System.out.println(product.toString()); }
```

How it works...

The AWS SDK internally calls the HTTP APIs to perform the operations. The scan operation scans the complete data in a DynamoDB table and filters out the result for you. If you have very large data in DynamoDB, then you should be very careful while using this operation as it might consume your entire provisioned read/write throughput.

There's more...

To make the scan faster on huge datasets, we can also perform parallel scans. To do so, we need to call the `parallelScan` method of the `mapper` class, specifying the number of parallel threads you want to execute for the scan. The syntax for this code is as follows:

```
PaginatedParallelScanList<Product> products = mapper.parallelScan(
    Product.class, scanExpression, 4);
  for (Product product : products) {
    System.out.println(product.toString());
}
```

Saving items into the DynamoDB table using the object persistence model in .Net

In the earlier recipes, we discussed how to use the object persistence model using Java; now, we will see how to use the object persistence model in .Net.

Getting ready

To perform this recipe, you should have set up the project, as described in the earlier recipes, specifically, `pom.xml`, dependencies, and the object model.

How to do it...

Let's see how to use the object persistence model in .Net:

1. Here, we will first create the `data` model and map the attributes to the attributes in a DynamoDB table. The .Net SDK provides built-in support for the object persistence model, so you don't need to do anything else. Annotations can be used to perform the mapping of data, as shown in the following code:

```
[DynamoDBTable("product")]
    public class Product
    {
        [DynamoDBHashKey]      // Hash key.
        public int id { get; set; }
        [DynamoDBRangeKey]     // Range key.
        public string type { get; set; }
        [DynamoDBProperty]
        public string name { get; set; }
        [DynamoDBProperty]
        public string mnfr { get; set; }
    }
```

2. Now we will create an instance of `AmazonDynamoDBClient` and instantiate the `DynamoDBContext` class, which will be the entry point to DynamoDB. The `DynamoDBContext` class will provide us a method to persist the data in DynamoDB:

```
AmazonDynamoDBClient client = new AmazonDynamoDBClient();
DynamoDBContext context = new DynamoDBContext(client);
```

3. Now, instantiate the object instance of the Product class and put the values into it, if required:

```
        Product product = new Product
            {
                id = 111,
                type = "book",
                name = "DynamoDB Cookbook",
                mnfr = "packtpub"
            };
```

4. Once done, we need to invoke the `Save()` method of the context class to persist the data in DynamoDB:

```
// Save the product.
  context.Save(product);
```

How it works...

The AWS SDK internally calls the HTTP APIs to perform the operations. In the object persistence model, the class is mapped to the DynamoDB table and each instance of the class is mapped to the row in the DynamoDB table.

There is more...

You can also perform the batch write operations using the object persistence model, as shown in the following code:

```
var productBatch = context.CreateBatchWrite<Product>();
 productBatch.AddPutItems(new List<Product> { product1, product2 });
```

Retrieving items from the DynamoDB table using the object persistence model in .Net

Now, we will see how to use the object persistence model in .Net to get the data from DynamoDB.

Getting ready

To perform this recipe, you should have set up the project, as described in the earlier recipes, specifically, `pom.xml`, dependencies, and the object model.

How to do it...

1. Create an instance of `AmazonDynamoDBClient` and instantiate the `DynamoDBContext` class, which will be the entry point to DynamoDB:

    ```
    AmazonDynamoDBClient client = new AmazonDynamoDBClient();
    DynamoDBContext context = new DynamoDBContext(client);
    ```

2. Invoke the load method from the `DynamoDBContext` class, specifying the keys of a DynamoDB item that you wish to retrieve:

    ```
    Product productRetrieved = context.Load<Product>(111, "book");
    ```

How it works...

The AWS SDK internally calls the HTTP APIs to perform the operations. The load method retrieves the data from DynamoDB and puts it into the object that we created. To retrieve a specific attribute of the item, we can use the getter methods of the object.

There is more...

Likewise, we can also invoke methods to update the items and delete them as well. For any updates, we have to use the `Save()` method. For the deletion, we can use the `Delete()` method of the DynamoDB mapper class. You may try this as well. Note that once the data has been deleted, there is no way to get it back, so use this method with care.

Creating a custom object for the DynamoDB table using the object persistence model in .Net

Now, we will see how to use the object persistence model in .Net to create a custom object.

Getting ready

To perform this recipe, you should have set up the project, as described in the earlier recipes, specifically, `pom.xml`, dependencies, and the object model.

How to do it...

The object persistence model for .Net only supports primitive data types to be used as attribute data types. But, sometimes, we might want to use some custom objects. In order to do so, we need to perform the following operations:

1. Declare the `product` class as we did earlier. We also need to create the custom `object` class and declare this class in the `product` class. In this case, we want to create an object that will help us store the dimensions of the product, and then it can be declared, as follows:

```
public class Dimension
    {
        public decimal Length { get; set; }
        public decimal Height { get; set; }
        public decimal Width { get; set; }
    }
```

2. Next, we declare an instance of this class as an attribute of the `product` class:

```
[DynamoDBTable("ProductCatalog")]
    public class Book
    {
        . . .
```

```
    [DynamoDBProperty(typeof(DimensionConverter))]
    public Dimension Dimensions { get; set; }
...
}
```

3. Here, we also need to write a `converter` class that knows how to read and write the attributes to and from DynamoDB. Even though we write these objects as custom objects, DynamoDB stores them as strings only:

```
public class DimensionConverter : IPropertyConverter
{
    public DynamoDBEntry ToEntry(object value)
    {
        DimensionType prodDimensions = value as DimensionType;
        string data = string.Format("{1}{0}{2}{0}{3}",
          " x ",
            prodDimensions.Length, prodDimensions.Height,
              prodDimensions.Width);

        DynamoDBEntry entry = new Primitive { Value =
          data };
        return entry;
    }

    public object FromEntry(DynamoDBEntry entry)
    {
        Primitive primitive = entry as Primitive;

        string[] data = ((string)(primitive.Value))
          .Split(new string[] { " x " },
            StringSplitOptions.None);
        if (data.Length != 3) throw new
          ArgumentOutOfRangeException();

        DimensionType dimensions = new DimensionType
        {
            Length = Convert.ToDecimal(data[0]),
            Height = Convert.ToDecimal(data[1]),
            Width = Convert.ToDecimal(data[2])
        };
        return dimensions;
    }
}
```

How it works...

Custom classes help us work with DynamoDB in a more natural way. When we put the data into the DynamoDB table, this custom object will be stored as a string, and while fetching, it reads the string and converts it to an object for better accessibility.

Querying items from the DynamoDB table using the object persistence model in .Net

Now, we are going to see how to query items from the table using the object persistence model in .Net

Getting ready

To perform this recipe, you should have set up the project, as described in the earlier recipes, specifically `pom.xml` and setting up dependencies and the object model.

How to do it...

Let's see how to query items from the table using the object persistence model in .Net:

1. Create an instance of `AmazonDynamoDBClient` and instantiate the `DynamoDBContext` class, which will be the entry point to DynamoDB:

    ```
    AmazonDynamoDBClient client = new AmazonDynamoDBClient();
    DynamoDBContext context = new DynamoDBContext(client);
    ```

2. Now, let's write a query that will fetch the items whose ID is 111 and type starts with b:

    ```
    IEnumerable<Product> products =
                context.Query<Product>(111, QueryOperator.BeginsWith,
    "b");
    ```

3. Now, we can iterate over the products' list to go through the results.

How it works...

The AWS SDK internally calls the HTTP APIs to perform the operations. Here, we are using "begins" with an operator, but depending on the query requirements, you can change the condition.

Scanning items from the DynamoDB table using the object persistence model in .Net

Now, we are going to see how to scan items from the table using the object persistence model in .Net.

Getting ready

To perform this recipe, you should have set up the project, as described in the earlier recipes, specifically, `pom.xml`, dependencies, and the object model.

How to do it...

1. Create an instance of `AmazonDynamoDBClient` and instantiate the `DynamoDBContext` class, which will be the entry point to DynamoDB:

   ```
   AmazonDynamoDBClient client = new AmazonDynamoDBClient();
   DynamoDBContext context = new DynamoDBContext(client);
   ```

2. Now, let's write a scan condition to fetch all the items whose type is book:

   ```
   context.Scan<Product>(
   new ScanCondition("type", ScanOperator.EqualTo, "book"));
   ```

3. Now, we can iterate over the products' list to go through the results.

How it works...

The AWS SDK internally calls the HTTP APIs to perform the operations. Here, we are using the equal to condition operator to fetch the results, but as per the query requirements, you can choose from the other condition operators.

6
Securing DynamoDB

In this chapter, we will cover the following topics:

- ▸ Creating users using AWS IAM
- ▸ Creating a DynamoDB full access group using AWS IAM
- ▸ Creating a DynamoDB read-only group using AWS IAM
- ▸ Validating the DynamoDB access controls using the AWS IAM policy simulator
- ▸ Creating the custom policy to allow the DynamoDB console access using AWS IAM
- ▸ Creating a fine-grained access control policy using AWS IAM
- ▸ Implementing the client-side encryption for the DynamoDB data
- ▸ Implementing the client-side masking for the DynamoDB data

Introduction

In the previous chapter, we explored high-level programming interfaces for DynamoDB. In this chapter, we will impose security on DynamoDB. We will see how to manage the DynamoDB access controls, how to create security policies, and so on. It is very important to control the data access when you are using DynamoDB in production to avoid the misuse.

For all access controls on DynamoDB, we will use the AWS **Identity and Access Management** (**IAM**) service. AWS IAM provides you the facility to create user groups and use permissions to allow or deny their access to certain resources. As we go through the recipes, we will be able to explore AWS IAM in more detail.

Here is a link to read more on AWS IAM at `https://aws.amazon.com/iam/`.

Creating users using AWS IAM

To get started with the identity and access control, the first step is to create users, which we will use for our next recipes.

Getting ready

To perform this recipe, you need to know how to access the DynamoDB console.

How to do it...

Let's create users using AW SIAM:

1. Log on to the AWS Console by providing the valid credentials at:
   `https://console.aws.amazon.com`.

2. Navigate to the AWS IAM service from the console dashboard. You will see the following screen:

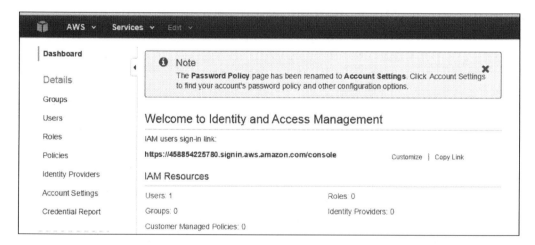

3. Click on the **Users** link from the left-hand side navigation pane. You will be directed to the **Users** page, where you can see the **Create New Users** button. Click on this button to create new users.

4. You will see a screen with some textboxes where you can provide the names of users to be created. Enter the names, and click on the **Create** button. The screen will also have one checkbox, which should be checked, in order to create the access and secret keys for the newly created users.

5. The next screen will provide an option for you to download the credentials for the newly created users. You may download these credentials and keep them for further use.

How it works...

AWS IAM users are nothing but subaccounts with which you can access your AWS resources. By default, these users will not have any access unless you explicitly provide those to them. The credentials that we generated will have an access key and a secret key separate for each user. These credentials should not be shared with any other person outside your trusted circle to avoid any misuse.

Creating a DynamoDB full access group using AWS IAM

Now that we have created the users, it's time to create groups and provide access controls to them.

Getting ready

To perform this recipe, you need to know how to access the DynamoDB console.

How to do it...

Let's create a DynamoDB with full access of group using AWS IAM:

1. Sign in to the AWS console and navigate to the IAM service.

2. You will see a **Create New Group** button, which allows you to create a new group. Click on this button to create one:

3. On the next screen, you will see a tab where you need to provide a group name, say `dynamodb-full-access-group`. Click on the **Next Step** button to continue.

4. In the following screenshot, we will need to attach a policy to that group; here, we are creating a group that has full access to the DynamoDB resources, so we will select the same policy. We can create a custom policy or use AWS predefined policies. We will discuss how to create a custom policy later in this chapter. For this recipe, we will use the predefined **AWS** policy `AmazonDynamoDBFullAccess`. Click on the `Next Step` button to attach the policy to the group.

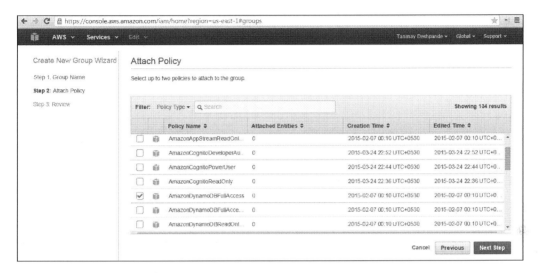

5. Next, you will see a screen to review the group name and attached policy. On confirmation, you can click on the **Create Group** button.

6. Once the group is created, we can add users to this group. To do so, place a check mark in the **Group Name** box, click on **Group Actions**, and then select the **Add users to Group** link, as shown in the following screenshot:

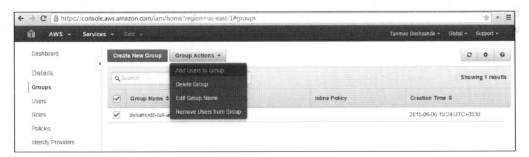

7. On the next screen, select the users to be added to the group, and click on the **Add Users** button.

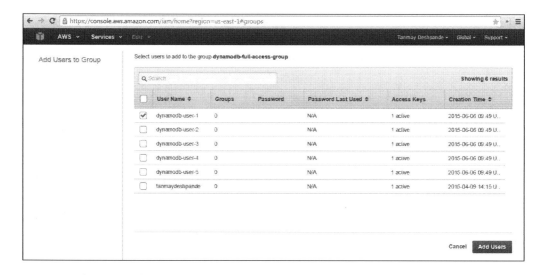

How it works...

It's always good to create groups and attach policies to the group instead of individual users. This allows you to easily maintain the access controls. Whenever we call any DynamoDB API along with the credentials, it first checks the privileges we have using AWS IAM. Any unauthorized access is blocked.

Creating a DynamoDB read-only group using AWS IAM

In this recipe, we will create a user group who will have a read-only access to DynamoDB.

Getting ready

To perform this recipe, you need to know how to access the DynamoDB console.

How to do it...

Let's create read-only group using AWS IAM;

1. Create a user group, as described in the previous recipe, with the name `dynamodb-read-only-group` and attach the `AmazonDynamoDBReadOnlyAccess` policy, as shown in the following screenshot:

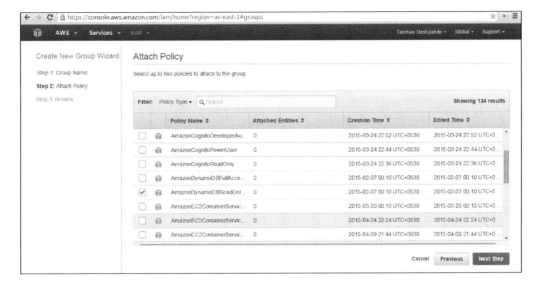

2. Once the group is created and the policy is attached to it, you may add users to the group. You can refer to the previous recipe for more details. Here, I am adding `dynamodb-user-2` to this group.

How it works...

The read-only policy allows users to only read the items; it does not allow users to modify any items. All write operations such as `PutItem`, `BatchWriteItems`, and so on are blocked. The users of this group can only perform the `GetItem`, `BatchGetItem`, `Query`, and `Scan` operations.

Validating the DynamoDB access controls using the AWS IAM policy simulator

It's always important to validate the security enforcement that we are going to impose on DynamoDB resources. In this recipe, we will see how to test the security features of DynamoDB.

Getting ready

To perform this recipe, you should have performed the earlier recipes.

How to do it...

Let's validate and test the security features of DynamoDB:

1. Go to the AWS IAM policy simulator. If you are already logged in to the AWS console on the browser, then you will be signed in to the simulator as well. You can refer to `https://policysim.aws.amazon.com` for more details.

2. Now, we want to test the access controls for the groups that we created in the earlier recipes. First, we will test the read-only group. For this, select the **Groups** tab from the drop-down menu, and click on **dynamodb-read-only-group**, which is to be tested, as shown in the following screenshot:

3. Next, select the **Service** button on which we want to test our controls, that is, DynamoDB. Select the **Action** to be performed, say `PutItem`, `BatchWriteItems`, `UpdateTable`, `DeleteItem`, and so on, which are all the write operations. Now, click on the **Run Simulation** button. You will see that all these operations are denied:

4. Now, let's try executing the same simulation using the full access group, and you will see that all these operations are allowed:

How it works...

The policy simulator helps us to verify the controls we impose with ease. It's always best practice to create controls, test these controls with a simulator, and only then impose them on production users. This way, we can be sure of the controls we apply. The AWS IAM simulator does not make any changes to your DynamoDB tables/items, so we can safely test those. It only checks whether a certain operation is permitted. We can test multiple operations in one go, as we did in our recipe.

Creating the custom policy to allow the DynamoDB console access using AWS IAM

In the earlier recipes, we learnt how to use the AWS defined policies to enforce access controls. Now, we will see how to create and apply the custom policy.

Getting ready

To perform this recipe, you should have performed the earlier recipes.

How to do it...

Let's create and apply custom policy:

1. Log on to the AWS IAM console, as we did in the earlier recipes. Go to the **Policies** section in the left-hand side navigation pane of your AWS IAM console. Click on the **Create Policy** button.

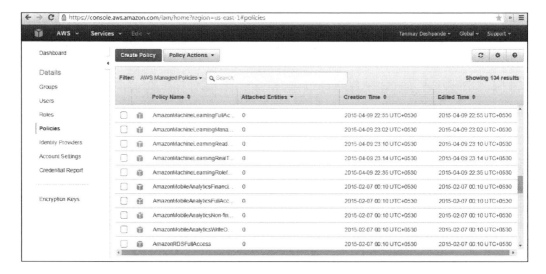

2. Next, you will see the policy creation screen, which will allow you to create a policy in three ways: in the first option, you can copy the managed policy and edit as per your preference; in the second option, you can use a policy generator, which will guide you to create the policy, and the third option will allow you to create your policy by writing the policy from scratch. Here, we will go with the second option, which is recommended to create unnecessary confusion if you are not aware of the document structure. Although, you may choose any option as per your convenience.

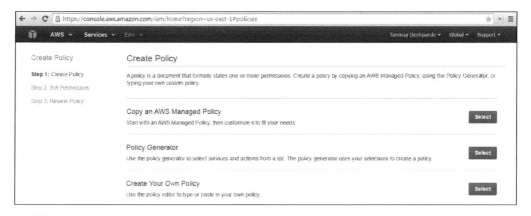

3. On the **Set Permissions** screen, you can choose the service and its permissions. The wizard is interactive so it's quite easy to use. Here, I want to create a policy that will allow the user/group to use the DynamoDB console. To do so, it needs the `DescribeTable` and `ListTables` actions from DynamoDB and the `DescribeAlarms` and `ListMetrics` actions from the CloudWatch service. You can click on the **Next Step** button once you add these statements.

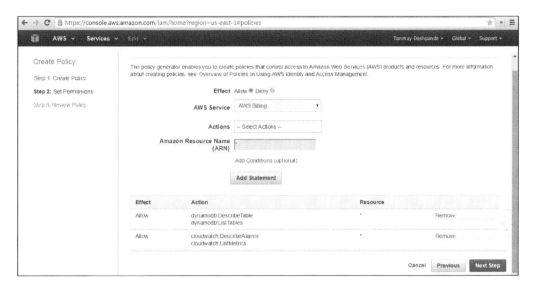

4. On the next screen, you can review the policy. We can provide a meaningful policy name and description, and click on the **Validate Policy** button. On validation, you can click on the **Create Policy** button.

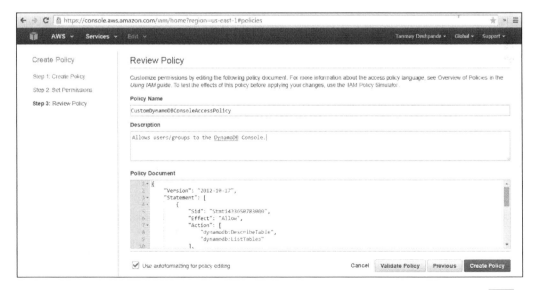

Here is how the policy statement looks:

```
{
    "Version": "2012-10-17",
    "Statement": [
        {
            "Sid": "Stmt1433650783000",
            "Effect": "Allow",
            "Action": [
                "dynamodb:DescribeTable",
                "dynamodb:ListTables"
            ],
            "Resource": [
                "*"
            ]
        },
        {
            "Sid": "Stmt1433650896000",
            "Effect": "Allow",
            "Action": [
                "cloudwatch:DescribeAlarms",
                "cloudwatch:ListMetrics"
            ],
            "Resource": [
                "*"
            ]
        }
    ]
}
```

5. Now, you can create a new group and attach this policy, as we did in the earlier recipes to see thing stake effect.

How it works...

The custom policy works in exactly the way AWS defines the policies. Whenever a client makes a call to DynamoDB with the security credentials, it first checks the permission it has, and then allows or denies the access. AWS has provided a very nice wizard to generate the policies, which helps users to enforce security with ease. You can also test any new policies created with a simulator, which we have seen in the earlier recipes.

Creating a fine-grained access control policy using AWS IAM

A fine-grained access control allows us to restrict access to the table data as we want it. It allows us to create policies, which allow users to access only their data, limit their access to certain attributes, and so on. In this recipe, we will see how to create a fine-grained policy.

Getting ready

To perform this recipe, you should have performed the earlier recipes.

How to do it...

Here, the policy creation actions will be similar to the earlier recipe. So, we will directly jump to the policy wizard set permissions screen. Here, we will consider the same e-commerce example that we have been considering since the start of this book, where we had a product table. If you want to hide certain attributes, such as purchase price and stock, from the end users, then you can create a policy that will deny access to these items:

1. Navigate to the create policy user interface, and select the third option, that is, **Create Your Own Policy**.

2. You may give a relevant name to the policy and describe the purpose of this policy. In the **Policy Document section**, you can write the policy, as shown in the following screenshot:

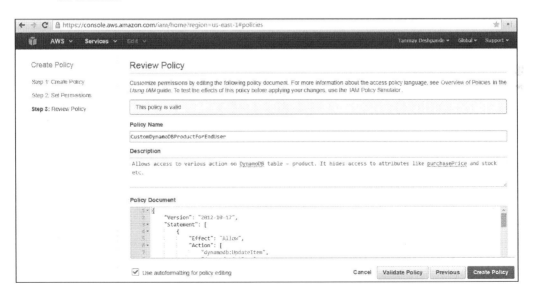

The complete policy document will look like this:

```
{
    "Version": "2012-10-17",
    "Statement": [{
        "Effect": "Allow",
        "Action": ["dynamodb:UpdateItem",
        "dynamodb:GetItem",
        "dynamodb:Query",
        "dynamodb:BatchGetItem",
        "dynamodb:Scan"],
        "Resource": ["arn:aws:dynamodb:
            us-east-1:458854225780:table/product"],
        "Condition": {
        "ForAllValues:StringEquals": {
            "dynamodb:Attributes": ["id",
                "type",
                "mnfr",
                "features",
                "name",
                "dimensions"]
            },
            "StringEqualsIfExists": {
                "dynamodb:Select": "SPECIFIC_ATTRIBUTES",
                "dynamodb:ReturnValues": ["NONE",
                "UPDATED_OLD",
                "UPDATED_NEW"]
            }
        }
    }]
}
```

3. For further details on the policy structure, you can refer to `http://docs.aws.amazon.com/IAM/latest/UserGuide/policies_overview.html`.

4. On validation, you can click on the **Create Policy** button, and then attach this policy to a specific user, group, or role.

How it works...

This policy limits the users to only perform read operations on given attributes. Here, we have not included items, such as `purchasePrice` and stock, as we want the end user to NOT be able to access these attributes. We have also not included any write operations, as write operations either create new items or replace the exiting items. The DynamoDB ARN can be found on the DynamoDB console under the **Details** section.

Implementing the client-side encryption for the DynamoDB data

It's been quite a long time since Cloud has been in production, but some people still have concerns about the security it provides. Also, it's always good to have additional levels of security to make sure that the data is safe. In order to do so, in this recipe, we are going to see how to encrypt data before saving it in a DynamoDB table.

Getting ready

To perform this recipe, you should know how to use the AWS SDK for Java, especially its object persistence model. Refer to *Chapter 5, Exploring Higher Level Programming Interfaces for DynamoDB,* for more details.

How to do it...

To get started with this recipe, we need to create a **maven** project and add the following dependencies to it:

1. Add dependencies to the AWS SDK for Java and the `aws-dynamodb-encryption-java` library:

   ```
   <dependency>

   <groupId>com.amazonaws</groupId>

     <artifactId>aws-java-sdk</artifactId>

     <version>1.9.34</version>

   </dependency>

   <dependency>

     <groupId>com.amazonaws</groupId>

     <artifactId>aws-dynamodb-encryption-java</artifactId>

     <version>0.0.3-SNAPSHOT</version>

   </dependency>
   ```

2. The `aws-dynamodb-encryption-java` library still needs to be downloaded from the snapshot release branch. So, in order to enable the snapshot release download, we need the following profile in `pom.xml`:

   ```
   <profiles>
     <profile>
   ```

```
      <id>allow-snapshots</id>
      <activation>
    <activeByDefault>true</activeByDefault>
      </activation>
    <repositories>
          <repository>
        <id>snapshots-repo</id>
    <url>https://oss.sonatype.org/content/repositories/
      snapshots</url>
            <releases>
              <enabled>false</enabled>
            </releases>
            <snapshots>
              <enabled>true</enabled>
            </snapshots>
          </repository>
        </repositories>
      </profile>
  </profiles>
```

3. Next, we need to create a `data model` for the items to be stored in DynamoDB, as we did in the previous chapter. Here, I am going to use the same product table. If you don't want all of your attributes to get encrypted, then you can use the `@ DonotEncrypt` annotation. Here, if I don't want the cost attribute to not encrypted, then I need to mark it as follows:

```
@DoNotEncrypt
@DynamoDBAttribute(attributeName = "cost")
public double getCost() {
  return cost;
}
```

4. Now, we need to write the code to put items in an encrypted form in DynamoDB. Here, I am using `KeyGenerator` from the Java security model to generate the encryption keys. We will need two secret keys: one is the encryption key and the other one is the signing key. Here is the code to generate the keys:

```
SecureRandom rnd = new SecureRandom();
KeyGenerator aesGen = null;
try {
  aesGen = KeyGenerator.getInstance("AES");
} catch (NoSuchAlgorithmException e1) {
  e1.printStackTrace();
}
aesGen.init(128, rnd);
SecretKey encryptionKey = aesGen.generateKey();
KeyGenerator macGen = null;
```

```
try {
  macGen = KeyGenerator.getInstance("HmacSHA256");
} catch (NoSuchAlgorithmException e) {
  e.printStackTrace();
}
macGen.init(256, rnd);
SecretKey macKey = macGen.generateKey();
```

Here, we are using various algorithms, such as AES and `HmacSHA256`, for the key generation. You can read more about KeyGenerator at `http://docs.oracle.com/javase/7/docs/api/javax/crypto/KeyGenerator.html`.

5. Now, we need to use these keys to initiate the encryption provider, as follows:

```
EncryptionMaterialsProvider provider = new SymmetricStaticProvider
(encryptionKey, macKey);
```

6. Now, we can initiate the DynamoDB client and the mapper class, and use them to persist the data:

```
AmazonDynamoDBClient client = new AmazonDynamoDBClient(
  new ProfileCredentialsProvider());
  client.setRegion(Region.getRegion(Regions.US_EAST_1));
DynamoDBMapper mapper = new DynamoDBMapper(client,
  DynamoDBMapperConfig.DEFAULT, new
AttributeEncryptor(provider));
  Product product = new Product();
    product.setId(1002);
    product.setType("book");
    product.setTitle("Hadoop Cookbook");
    product.setMnfr("PacktPub");
    product.setCost(43.99);
    mapper.save(product);
```

7. Invoke the method, and you will be able to see the encrypted data saved in the DynamoDB table:

Here, you can see all the attributes except keys and `cost` that are encrypted. This library also makes sure that while fetching the data from DynamoDB, it gets decrypted at the client, and we can see the unencrypted data. The only thing that we need to make sure of is that we have to use the same keys for encryption and decryption.

How it works...

The encryption library encrypts the data before sending it over the network to DynamoDB. It uses the Java recommended encryption technology, so we are sure of the level of security of the encryption. One thing to note here is that JDK/JRE does not support built-in support for **Java Cryptography Extension** (**JCE**), so you need to download JAR from `http://www.oracle.com/technetwork/java/javase/downloads/jce8-download-2133166.html` and copy them to `/path-to/jre/lib/security`.

If you are using an older version of JDK/JRE, then you should download the correct JCE from the Oracle website from `http://www.oracle.com/technetwork/java/javase/downloads/index.html`.

Implementing the client-side masking for the DynamoDB data

Similar to the requirements from the previous recipe, there might be a need to mask data before saving it in DynamoDB. Masking is replacing real data with realistic data for sensitive information, such as names, dates of birth, **Social Security number** (**SSN**), credit/debit card numbers, and so on. Generally, when it comes to the security of testing data, people prefer masking over encryption. In this recipe, we will see how to mask such data before saving it in DynamoDB.

Getting ready

To perform this recipe, you should know how to use the AWS SDK for Java, especially its object persistence model. Refer to Chapter 5, *Exploring Higher Level Programming Interfaces for DynamoDB*, for more details.

How to do it...

Unlike encryption, AWS does not provide support for data masking, so we need to use custom solutions for masking the data before storing it in DynamoDB.

Consider our e-commerce website where we save our customer's credit card details. Here, let's assume for some reason, that we have to give this data to some other team for testing. Now, we cannot give the actual data to them as it might be a security risk, and we also cannot give them the encrypted data as it might not be of use to them. So, it's good to mask this data.

Let's implement the client-side masking for the DynamoDB data:

1. To get started, we will use the AWS Java SDK to insert an item into a customer table. Here, we will initiate the DynamoDB client with the correct credentials:

```
AmazonDynamoDBClient client = new AmazonDynamoDBClient(
    new ProfileCredentialsProvider());
  client.setRegion(Region.getRegion(Regions.US_EAST_1));
DynamoDB dynamoDB = new DynamoDB(client);
Table table = dynamoDB.getTable("customer");
```

2. Now, we can write some custom masking algorithms to mask the credit card number before saving it in DynamoDB. Here, I have written one simple algorithm, which expects the CC number in the format `1111-2222-3333-4444`. First, it splits the string by `-`, then on each, a four digit number is subtracted from `9999` to get the masked number. So, using this algorithm, the preceding CC number will be masked as `8888-7777-6666-5555`:

```
private static String maskCCNo(String ccNo) {
  StringBuilder sb = new StringBuilder();
  String[] ccParts = ccNo.split("[-]");
  for (int i = 0; i < ccParts.length; i++) {
    int ccPartInt = Integer.parseInt(ccParts[i]);
    sb.append(9999 - ccPartInt);
    if (i != 3) {
    sb.append("-");
  }
}
}
    return sb.toString();
  }
```

3. We can use the preceding code to mask the credit card information and save the data in DynamoDB:

```
String ccNo = "5996-5887-8980-6971";
String maskedccNo = maskCCNo(ccNo);
System.out.println("Masked CC No :" + maskedccNo);
Item customer = new Item().withPrimaryKey(new
  PrimaryKey("id", 1000))
.withString("name", "James Bond").withString("ccNo", ccNo);
  PutItemOutcome outcome = table.putItem(customer);
```

How it works...

Masking is good if you want to use DynamoDB for some testing. It does not save the real data but the realistic data. Realistic data is generally in the same format as the real data, whereas encrypted data is completely different to the original data. Masking algorithms can vary depending on the complexity of your use case. For complex credit card masking algorithms, you should first learn about Luhn's Algorithm. You can be find more details at `http://en.wikipedia.org/wiki/Luhn_algorithm`.

7

DynamoDB Best Practices

In this chapter, we will cover the following topics:

- ► Using a standalone cache for frequently accessed items
- ► Using the AWS ElastiCache for frequently accessed items
- ► Compressing large data before storing it in DynamoDB
- ► Using AWS S3 for storing large items
- ► Catching DynamoDB errors
- ► Performing auto-retries on DynamoDB errors
- ► Performing atomic transactions on DynamoDB tables
- ► Performing asynchronous requests to DynamoDB

Introduction

In the previous chapter, we discussed how to impose security constraints to secure the data. In this chapter, we are going to talk about DynamoDB implementation best practices, which will help you improve the performance while reducing the operation cost. So, let's get started.

Using a standalone cache for frequently accessed items

In this recipe, we will see how to use a standalone cache for frequently accessed items. A cache is a temporary data store that will save the items in memory and will provide those from the memory itself instead of making a DynamoDB call. Make a note that this should be used for items, which you expect to not be changed frequently.

Getting ready

We will perform this recipe using Java libraries. So, the prerequisite is that you should have performed recipes, which use the AWS SDK for Java.

How to do it...

Here, we will be using the AWS SDK for Java, so create a Maven project with the SDK dependency. Apart from the SDK, we will also be using one of the most widely used open source caches, that is, EhCache. To know about EhCache, refer to http://ehcache.org/.

Let's use a standalone cache for frequently accessed items:

1. To use EhCache, we need to include the following repository in pom.xml:

```
<repositories>
  <repository>
    <id>sourceforge</id>
    <name>sourceforge</name>
    <url>https://oss.sonatype.org/content/repositories/
      sourceforge-releases/</url>
  </repository>
</repositories>
```

2. We will also need to add the following dependency:

```
<dependency>
  <groupId>net.sf.ehcache</groupId>
  <artifactId>ehcache</artifactId>
  <version>2.9.0</version>
</dependency>
```

3. Once the project setup is done, we will create a cachemanager class, which will be used in the following code:

```
public class ProductCacheManager {
  // Ehcache cache manager
  CacheManager cacheManager = CacheManager.getInstance();
```

```
      private Cache productCache;
      public Cache getProductCache() {
        return productCache;
      }
      //Create an instance of cache using cache manager
      public ProductCacheManager() {
        cacheManager.addCache("productCache");
        this.productCache = cacheManager.getCache("productCache");
      }
      public void shutdown() {
        cacheManager.shutdown();
      }
    }
```

4. Now, we will create another class where we will write a code to get the item from DynamoDB. Here, we will first initiate the `ProductCacheManager`:

```
static ProductCacheManager cacheManager = new
ProductCacheManager();
```

5. Next, we will write a method to get the item from DynamoDB. Before we fetch the data from DynamoDB, we will first check whether the item with the given key is available in the cache. If it is available in cache, we will return it from the cache itself. If the item is not found in the cache, we will first fetch it from DynamoDB and immediately put it into the cache. Once the item is cached, every time we need this item, we will get it from the cache, unless the cached item is evicted:

```
private static Item getItem(int id, String type) {
    Item product = null;
    if (cacheManager.getProductCache().isKeyInCache(id + ":" +
type)) {
    Element prod = cacheManager.getProductCache().get(id + ":" +
type);
    product = (Item) prod.getObjectValue();
    System.out.println("Returning from Cache");
    } else {
      AmazonDynamoDBClient client = new AmazonDynamoDBClient(
        new ProfileCredentialsProvider());
      client.setRegion(Region.getRegion(Regions.US_EAST_1));
      DynamoDB dynamoDB = new DynamoDB(client);
      Table table = dynamoDB.getTable("product");
      product = table.getItem(new PrimaryKey("id", id, "type",
type));
      cacheManager.getProductCache().put(
        new Element(id + ":" + type, product));
      System.out.println("Making DynamoDB Call for getting the
item");
```

```
    }
    return product;
}
```

6. Now we can use this method whenever needed. Here is how we can test it:

```
Item product = getItem(10, "book");
System.out.println("First call :Item: " + product);
Item product1 = getItem(10, "book");
System.out.println("Second call :Item: " + product1);
cacheManager.shutdown();
```

How it works...

EhCache is one of the most popular standalone caches used in the industry. Here, we are using `EhCache` to store frequently accessed items from the `product` table. Cache keeps all its data in memory. Here, we will save every item against its keys that are cached. We have the product table, which has the composite hash and range keys, so we will also store the items against the key of (Hash Key and Range Key).

Note that caching should be used for only those tables that expect lesser updates. It should only be used for the table that holds static data. If anyone uses the cache for tables that are not static, then you will get stale data. You can also go to the next level and implement a time-based cache, which holds the data for a certain time, and after that, it clears the cache. We can also implement algorithms, such as **Least Recently Used** (**LRU**), **First In First Out** (**FIFO**), to make the cache more efficient.

Here, we will make comparatively lesser calls to DynamoDB, and ultimately, save some cost for ourselves.

Using the AWS ElastiCache for frequently accessed items

In this recipe, we will do the same thing that we did in the previous recipe. The only thing that we will change is that we will use a cloud hosted distributed caching solution instead of saving it on the local standalone cache.

ElastiCache is a hosted caching solution provided by Amazon Web Services. We have two options to select which caching technology you will need. One option is *Memcached*, and another option is *Redis*. Depending upon your requirements, you can decide which one to use. Here are links that will help you with more information on the two options:

▶ http://memcached.org/
▶ http://redis.io/

Getting ready

To get started with this recipe, we will need to have an ElastiCache cluster launched. If you are not aware of how to do it, you can refer to

```
http://aws.amazon.com/elasticache/.
```

How to do it...

Here, I am using the Memcached cluster. You can choose the size of the instance as you wish. We will need a Memcached client to access the cluster. Amazon has provided a compiled version of the Memcached client, which can be downloaded from `https://github.com/amazonwebservices/aws-elasticache-cluster-client-memcached-for-java`.

Once the JAR download is complete, you can add it to your Java Project class path:

1. To start with, we will need to get the configuration endpoint of the Memcached cluster that we launched. This configuration endpoint can be found on the AWS ElastiCache console itself. Here is how we can save the configuration endpoint and port:

```
static String configEndpoint = "my-elastic-
   cache.mlvymb.cfg.usw2.cache.amazonaws.com";
   static Integer clusterPort = 11211;
```

2. Similarly, we can instantiate the Memcached client:

```
static MemcachedClient client;
static {
  try {
    client = new MemcachedClient(new
      InetSocketAddress(configEndpoint, clusterPort));
    } catch (IOException e) {
    e.printStackTrace();
  }
}
```

3. Now, we can write the `getItem` method as we did for the previous recipe. Here, we will first check whether the item is present in the cache; if not, we will fetch it from DynamoDB, and put it into the cache. If the same request comes the next time, we will return it from the cache itself. While putting the item into the cache, we are also going to enter the expiry time of the item. We are going to set it to 3,600 seconds; that is, after 1 hour, the key entry will be deleted automatically:

```
private static Item getItem(int id, String type) {
    Item product = null;
    if (null != client.get(id + ":" + type)) {
      System.out.println("Returning from Cache");
```

```
      return (Item) client.get(id + ":" + type);
   } else {
      AmazonDynamoDBClient client = new
      AmazonDynamoDBClient(
         new ProfileCredentialsProvider());
   client.setRegion(Region.getRegion(Regions.US_EAST_1));
   DynamoDB dynamoDB = new DynamoDB(client);
   Table table = dynamoDB.getTable("product");
   product = table.getItem(new PrimaryKey("id", id,
      "type", type));
   System.out.println("Making DynamoDB Call for getting
      the item");
   ElasticCache.client.add(id + ":" + type, 3600,
      product);
   }
   return product;
}
```

How it works...

A distributed cache also works in the same fashion as a local one. A standalone cache keeps the data in memory and returns it if it finds the key. In a distributed cache, we have multiple nodes; here, keys are kept in a distributed manner. The distributed nature helps you divide the keys based on the hash value of the keys. So, when any request comes, it is redirected to a specified node and the value is returned from there.

Note that ElastiCache will help you provide a faster retrieval of items at the additional cost of the ElastiCache cluster. Also note that the preceding code will work if you execute the application from the EC2 instance only. If you try to execute this on the local machine, you will get connection errors.

Compressing large data before storing it in DynamoDB

We are all aware of DynamoDB's storage limitations for the item's size. Suppose that we get into a situation where storing large attributes in an item is a must. In that case, it's always a good choice to compress these attributes, and then save them in DynamoDB. In this recipe, we are going to see how to compress large items before storing them.

Getting ready

To get started with this recipe, you should have your workstation ready with Eclipse or any other IDE of your choice.

How to do it...

There are numerous algorithms with which we can compress the large items, for example, GZIP, LZO, BZ2, and so on. Each algorithm has a trade-off between the compression time and rate. So, it's your choice whether to go with a faster algorithm or with an algorithm, that provides a higher compression rate.

Consider a scenario in our e-commerce website, where we need to save the product reviews written by various users. For this, we created a `ProductReviews` table, where we will save the reviewer's name, its detailed product review, and the time when the review was submitted. Here, there is a chance that the product review messages will be large, and it would not be a good idea to store them as they are. So, it is important to understand how to compress these messages before storing them.

Let's see how to compress large data:

1. First of all, we will write a method that accepts the string input and returns the compressed byte buffer. Here, we are using the `GZIP` algorithm for compressions. Java has a built-in support, so we don't need to use any third-party library for this:

```
private static ByteBuffer compressString(String input)
        throws UnsupportedEncodingException, IOException {
  // Write the input as GZIP output stream using UTF-8 encoding
  ByteArrayOutputStream baos = new ByteArrayOutputStream();
  GZIPOutputStream os = new GZIPOutputStream(baos);
  os.write(input.getBytes("UTF-8"));
  os.finish();
  byte[] compressedBytes = baos.toByteArray();
    // Writing bytes to byte buffer
  ByteBuffer buffer = ByteBuffer.allocate(compressedBytes.length);
  buffer.put(compressedBytes, 0, compressedBytes.length);
  buffer.position(0);
  return buffer;
}
```

2. Now, we can simply use this method to store the data before saving it in DynamoDB. Here is an example of how to use this method in our code:

```
private static void putReviewItem() throws
    UnsupportedEncodingException, IOException {
  AmazonDynamoDBClient client = new AmazonDynamoDBClient(
    new ProfileCredentialsProvider());
  client.setRegion(Region.getRegion(Regions.US_EAST_1));
  DynamoDB dynamoDB = new DynamoDB(client);
  Table table = dynamoDB.getTable("ProductReviews");
  Item product = new Item()
    .withPrimaryKey(new PrimaryKey("id", 10))
      .withString("reviewerName", "John White")
        .withString("dateTime", "20-06-2015T08:09:30")
          .withBinary("reviewMessage",
            compressString("My Review Message"));
  PutItemOutcome outcome = table.putItem(product);
  System.out.println(outcome.getPutItemResult());
}
```

3. In a similar way, we can write a method that decompresses the data on retrieval from DynamoDB. Here is an example:

```
private static String uncompressString(ByteBuffer input) throws
    IOException {
  byte[] bytes = input.array();
  ByteArrayInputStream bais = new ByteArrayInputStream(bytes);
  ByteArrayOutputStream baos = new ByteArrayOutputStream();
  GZIPInputStream is = new GZIPInputStream(bais);
  int chunkSize = 1024;
  byte[] buffer = new byte[chunkSize];
  int length = 0;
  while ((length = is.read(buffer, 0, chunkSize)) != -1) {
    baos.write(buffer, 0, length);
  }
  return new String(baos.toByteArray(), "UTF-8");
}
```

How it works...

Compressing data at client side has numerous advantages. A smaller size means a lesser use of network and disk resources. Compression algorithms generally maintain a dictionary of words. While compressing, if they see the words getting repeated, then those words are replaced by their positions in the dictionary. In this way, the redundant data is eliminated and only their references are kept in the compressed string. While uncompressing the same data, the word references are replaced with the actual words, and we get our normal string back.

Various compression algorithms contain various compression techniques. Therefore, the compression algorithm that you choose will depend on your need.

Using AWS S3 for storing large items

Sometimes, we might get into a situation where storing data in a compressed format might not be sufficient enough. Consider a case where we might need to store large images or binaries that might exceed the DynamoDB's storage limitation per items. In this case, we can use AWS S3 to store such items and only save the S3 location in our DynamoDB table.

AWS S3: Simple Storage Service allows us to store data in a cheaper and efficient manner. To know more about AWS S3, you can visit

```
http://aws.amazon.com/s3/.
```

Getting ready

To get started with this recipe, you should have your workstation ready with the Eclipse IDE.

How to do it...

Consider a case in our e-commerce website where we would like to store the product images along with the product data. So, we will save the images on AWS S3, and only store their locations along with the product information in the product table:

1. First of all, we will see how to store data in AWS S3. For this, we need to go to the AWS console, and create an S3 bucket. Here, I created a bucket called e-commerce-product-images, and inside this bucket, I created folders to store the images. For example, /phone/apple/iphone6.

2. Now, let's write the code to upload the images to S3:

```
private static void uploadFileToS3() {
    String bucketName = "e-commerce-product-images";
    String keyName = "phone/apple/iphone6/iphone.jpg";
    String uploadFileName = "C:\\tmp\\iphone.jpg";
    // Create an instance of S3 client
    AmazonS3 s3client = new AmazonS3Client(new
        ProfileCredentialsProvider());
    // Start the file uploading
    File file = new File(uploadFileName);
    s3client.putObject(new PutObjectRequest(bucketName,
        keyName, file));
}
```

3. Once the file is uploaded, you can save its path in one of the attributes of the product table, as follows:

```
private static void putItemWithS3Link() {
    AmazonDynamoDBClient client = new AmazonDynamoDBClient(
        new ProfileCredentialsProvider());
    client.setRegion(Region.getRegion(Regions.US_EAST_1));
    DynamoDB dynamoDB = new DynamoDB(client);
    Table table = dynamoDB.getTable("productTable");
    Map<String, String> features = new HashMap<String, String>();
    features.put("camera", "13MP");
    features.put("intMem", "16GB");
    features.put("processor", "Dual-Core 1.4 GHz Cyclone
        (ARM v8-based)");

    Set<String> imagesSet = new HashSet<String>();
    imagesSet.add("https://s3-us-west-2.amazonaws.com/
        e-commerce-product-images/phone/apple/iphone6/iphone.jpg");
    Item product = new Item()
        .withPrimaryKey(new PrimaryKey("id", 250, "type", "phone"))
        .withString("mnfr", "Apple").withNumber("stock", 15)
        .withString("name", "iPhone 6").withNumber("price", 45)
        .withMap("features", features)
        .withStringSet("productImages", imagesSet);
    PutItemOutcome outcome = table.putItem(product);
    System.out.println(outcome.getPutItemResult());
}
```

4. So, whenever required, we can fetch the item by its key, and fetch the actual images from S3 using the URL saved in the `productImages` attribute.

How it works...

AWS S3 provides storage services at much cheaper rates. It's like a flat data dumping ground where we can store any type of file. So, it's always a good option to store large datasets in S3 and only keep its URL references in DynamoDB attributes. The URL reference will be the connecting link between the DynamoDB item and the S3 file.

If your file is too large to be sent in one S3 client call, you may want to explore its multipart API, which allows you to send the file in chunks.

Catching DynamoDB errors

Until now, we discussed how to perform various operations in DynamoDB. We saw how to use AWS provided by SDK and play around with DynamoDB items and attributes. Amazon claims that AWS provides high availability and reliability, which is quite true considering the years of experience I have gained from using their services, but we still cannot deny the possibility where services such as DynamoDB might not perform as expected. So, it's important to make sure that we have a proper error catching mechanism to ensure that the disaster recovery system is in place. In this recipe, we are going to see how to catch such errors.

Getting ready

To get started with this recipe, you should have your workstation ready with the Eclipse IDE.

How to do it...

Catching errors in DynamoDB is quite easy. Whenever we perform any operations, we need to put them in the `try` block. Along with it, we need to put a couple of catch blocks in order to catch the errors.

Here, we will consider a simple operation to put an item into the DynamoDB table. We have already seen how to do so in the earlier chapters:

```
try {
AmazonDynamoDBClient client = new AmazonDynamoDBClient(
  new ProfileCredentialsProvider());
client.setRegion(Region.getRegion(Regions.US_EAST_1));
DynamoDB dynamoDB = new DynamoDB(client);
Table table = dynamoDB.getTable("productTable");
Item product = new Item()
    .withPrimaryKey(new PrimaryKey("id", 10, "type", "mobile"))
    .withString("mnfr", "Samsung").withNumber("stock", 15)
    .withBoolean("isProductionStopped", true)
    .withNumber("price", 45);
PutItemOutcome outcome = table.putItem(product);
System.out.println(outcome.getPutItemResult());
} catch (AmazonServiceException ase) {
```

```
      System.out.println("Error Message: " + ase.getMessage());
      System.out.println("HTTP Status Code: " + ase.getStatusCode());
      System.out.println("AWS Error Code: " + ase.getErrorCode());
      System.out.println("Error Type: " + ase.getErrorType());
      System.out.println("Request ID: " + ase.getRequestId());
      } catch (AmazonClientException e) {
      System.out.println("Amazon Client Exception :" + e.getMessage());
   }
```

We should first catch `AmazonServiceException`, which arrives if the service you are trying to access throws any exception. `AmazonClientException` should be put last in order to catch any client-related exceptions.

How it works...

Amazon assigns a unique request ID for each and every request that it receives. Keeping this request ID is very important if something goes wrong, and if you would like to know what happened, then this request ID is the only source of information. We need to contact Amazon to know more about the request ID.

There are two types of errors in AWS:

  ▶ **Client errors**: These errors normally occur when the request we submit is incorrect. The client errors are normally shown with a status code starting with 4XX. These errors normally occur when there is an authentication failure, bad requests, missing required attributes, or for exceeding the provisioned throughput. These errors normally occur when users provide invalid inputs.

  ▶ **Server errors**: These errors occur when there is something wrong from Amazon's side and they occur at runtime. The only way to handle such errors is retries, and if they do not succeed, you should log the request ID, and then you can reach the Amazon support with that ID to know more about the details.

You can read more about DynamoDB specific errors at `http://docs.aws.amazon.com/amazondynamodb/latest/developerguide/ErrorHandling.html`.

Performing auto-retries on DynamoDB errors

As mentioned in the previous recipe, we can perform auto-retries on DynamoDB requests if we get errors. In this recipe, we are going to see how to perform auto-retries.

Getting ready

To get started with this recipe, you should have your workstation ready with the Eclipse IDE.

How to do it...

Auto-retries are required if we get any errors during the first request. We can use the Amazon client configurations to set our retry strategy. By default, the DynamoDB client auto-retries a request if any error is generated three times. If we think that this is not efficient for us, then we can define this on our own, as follows:

1. First of all, we need to create a custom implementation of `RetryCondition`. It contains a method called `shouldRetry`, which we need to implement as per our needs. Here is a sample `CustomRetryCondition` class:

```
public class CustomRetryCondition implements RetryCondition {
   public boolean shouldRetry(AmazonWebServiceRequest
originalRequest,
      AmazonClientException exception, int retriesAttempted) {
    if (retriesAttempted < 3 && exception.isRetryable()) {
      return true;
    } else {
      return false;
    }
   }
}
```

2. Similarly, we can implement `CustomBackoffStrategy`. The back-off strategy gives a hint on after what time the request should be retried. You can choose either a flat back-off time or an exponential back-off time:

```
public class CustomBackoffStrategy implements BackoffStrategy {
   /** Base sleep time (milliseconds) **/
   private static final int SCALE_FACTOR = 25;
   /** Maximum exponential back-off time before retrying a request
*/
   private static final int MAX_BACKOFF_IN_MILLISECONDS = 20 *
1000;
   public long delayBeforeNextRetry(AmazonWebServiceRequest
     originalRequest, AmazonClientException exception,
       int retriesAttempted) {
```

```
        if (retriesAttempted < 0)
        return 0;
        long delay = (1 << retriesAttempted) * SCALE_FACTOR;
        delay = Math.min(delay, MAX_BACKOFF_IN_MILLISECONDS);
        return delay;
    }
}
```

3. Next, we need to create an instance of `RetryPolicy` and set the `RetryCondition` and `BackoffStrategy` classes, which we created. Apart from this, we can also set a maximum number of retries. The last parameter is `honorMaxErrorRetryInClientConfig`; it defines whether this retry policy should honor the maximum error retry set by `ClientConfiguration.setMaxErrorRetry(int)`:

```
RetryPolicy retryPolicy = new RetryPolicy(customRetryCondition,
    customBackoffStrategy, 3, false);
```

4. Now, initiate the `ClientConfiguration`, and set the `RetryPolicy` that we created earlier:

```
ClientConfiguration clientConfiguration = new
ClientConfiguration();
clientConfiguration.setRetryPolicy(retryPolicy);
```

5. Now, we need to set this client configuration when we initiate the `AmazonDynamoDBClient`, and once done, your retry policy with a custom back-off strategy will be in place:

```
AmazonDynamoDBClient client = new AmazonDynamoDBClient(
    new ProfileCredentialsProvider(), clientConfiguration);
```

How it works...

Auto-retries are quite handy when we receive a sudden burst in DynamoDB requests. If there are more number of requests than the provisioned throughputs, then auto-retries with an exponential back-off strategy will definitely help in handling the load. So, if the client gets an exception, then it will get auto retried after sometime; if by then the load is less, then there wouldn't be any loss for your application.

The Amazon DynamoDB client uses `HttpClient` internally to make calls, which is quite a popular and reliable implementation. So, if you need to handle such cases, this kind of an implementation is a must.

In case of batch operations, if any failure occurs, DynamoDB does not fail the complete operation. In case of batch write operations or, if a particular operation fails, then DynamoDB returns the unprocessed items, which can be retried.

Performing atomic transactions on DynamoDB tables

I hope that we are all aware that operations in DynamoDB are eventually consistent. Considering this nature, it obviously does not support transactions the way we do in RDBMS. A transaction is a group of operations that need to be performed in one go, and they should be handled in an atomic nature. (If one operation fails, the complete transaction should be rolled back.)

There might be use cases where you would need to perform transactions in your application. Considering this need, AWS has provided open sources, client-side transaction libraries, which help us achieve atomic transactions in DynamoDB. In this recipe, we are going to see how to perform transactions on DynamoDB.

Getting ready

To get started with this recipe, you should have your workstation ready with the Eclipse IDE.

How to do it...

To get started, we will first need to download the source code of the library from GitHub and build the code to generate the JAR file. You can download the code from `https://github.com/awslabs/dynamodb-transactions/archive/master.zip`.

Next, extract the code and run the following command to generate the JAR file:

```
mvn clean install –DskipTests
```

On a successful build, you will see a JAR generated file in the target folder. Add this JAR to the project by choosing a configure build path in Eclipse:

1. Now, let's understand how to use transactions. For this, we need to create the DynamoDB client and help this client to create two `helper` tables. The first table would be the `Transactions` table to store the transactions, while the second table would be the `TransactionImages` table to keep the snapshots of the items modified in the transaction:

```
AmazonDynamoDBClient client = new AmazonDynamoDBClient(
  new ProfileCredentialsProvider());
  client.setRegion(Region.getRegion(Regions.US_EAST_1));
  // Create transaction table
  TransactionManager.verifyOrCreateTransactionTable(client,
    "Transactions", 10, 10, (long) (10 * 60));
  // Create transaction images table
  TransactionManager.verifyOrCreateTransactionImagesTable(client,
    "TransactionImages", 10, 10, (long) (60 * 10));
```

2. Next, we need to create a transaction manager by providing the names of the tables we created earlier:

```
TransactionManager txManager = new TransactionManager(client,
   "Transactions", "TransactionImages");
```

3. Now, we create one `transaction`, and perform the operations you will need to do in one go. Consider our `product` table where we need to add two new products in one single transaction; the changes will reflect only if both the operations are successful. We can perform these using transactions, as follows:

```
Transaction t1 = txManager.newTransaction();
Map<String, AttributeValue> product = new HashMap<String,
AttributeValue>();
AttributeValue id = new AttributeValue();
id.setN("250");
product.put("id", id);
product.put("type", new AttributeValue("phone"));
product.put("name", new AttributeValue("MI4"));
t1.putItem(new PutItemRequest("productTable", product));

Map<String, AttributeValue> product1 = new HashMap<String,
AttributeValue>();
id.setN("350");
product1.put("id", id);
product1.put("type", new AttributeValue("phone"));
product1.put("name", new AttributeValue("MI3"));
t1.putItem(new PutItemRequest("productTable", product1));
t1.commit();
```

4. Now, execute the code to see the results. If everything goes fine, you will see two new entries in the product table. In case of an error, none of the entries would be in the table.

How it works...

The transaction library when invoked, first writes the changes to the `Transaction` table, and then to the actual table. If we perform any update item operation, then it keeps the old values of that item in the `TransactionImages` table. It also supports multi-attribute and multi-table transactions. This way, we can use the transaction library and perform atomic writes. It also supports isolated reads. You can refer to the code and examples for more details at `https://github.com/awslabs/dynamodb-transactions`.

Performing asynchronous requests to DynamoDB

Until now, we have used a synchronous DynamoDB client to make requests to DynamoDB. Synchronous requests block the thread unless the operation is not performed. Due to network issues, sometimes it can be difficult for the operation to get completed quickly. In that case, we can go for asynchronous client requests so that we submit the requests and do some other work.

Getting ready

To get started with this recipe, you should have your workstation ready with the Eclipse IDE.

How to do it...

Asynchronous client is easy to use:

1. First, we need to instantiate the `AmazonDynamoDBAsync` class:

    ```
    AmazonDynamoDBAsync dynamoDBAsync = new AmazonDynamoDBAsyncClient(
        new ProfileCredentialsProvider());
    ```

2. Next, we need to create the request to be performed in an asynchronous manner. Let's say that we need to delete a certain item from our product table. Then, we can create the `DeleteItemRequest`, as shown in the following code snippet:

    ```
    Map<String, AttributeValue> key = new HashMap<String,
    AttributeValue>();
    AttributeValue id = new AttributeValue();
    id.setN("10");
    key.put("id", id);
    key.put("type", new AttributeValue("phone"));
    DeleteItemRequest deleteItemRequest = new DeleteItemRequest(
        "productTable", key);
    ```

3. Next, invoke the `deleteItemAsync` method to delete the item. Here, we can optionally define `AsyncHandler` if we want to use the result of the request we had invoked. Here, I am also printing the messages with time so that we can confirm its asynchronous nature:

    ```
    dynamoDBAsync.deleteItemAsync(deleteItemRequest,
        new AsyncHandler<DeleteItemRequest, DeleteItemResult>() {
        public void onSuccess(DeleteItemRequest request,
            DeleteItemResult result) {
    ```

```
        System.out.println("Item deleted successfully: "+
          System.currentTimeMillis());
      }
      public void onError(Exception exception) {
        System.out.println("Error deleting item in async way");
      }
    });
    System.out.println("Delete item initiated" +
      System.currentTimeMillis());
```

How it works

Asynchronous clients use `AsyncHttpClient` to invoke the DynamoDB APIs. This is a wrapper implementation on top of Java asynchronous APIs. Hence, they are quite easy to use and understand. The `AsyncHandler` is an optional configuration you can do in order to use the results of asynchronous calls. We can also use the Java `Future` object to handle the response.

8

Integrating DynamoDB with other AWS Services

In this chapter, we will cover the following topics:

- ▶ Importing data from AWS S3 to DynamoDB using AWS Data Pipeline
- ▶ Exporting data from AWS S3 to DynamoDB using AWS Data Pipeline
- ▶ Accessing the DynamoDB data using AWS EMR
- ▶ Querying the DynamoDB data using AWS EMR
- ▶ Performing join operations on the DynamoDB data using AWS EMR
- ▶ Exporting data to AWS S3 from DynamoDB using AWS EMR
- ▶ Logging DynamoDB operations using AWS CloudTrail
- ▶ Exporting the DynamoDB data to AWS Redshift
- ▶ Importing the DynamoDB data to AWS CloudSearch
- ▶ Performing a full text search on the DynamoDB data using CloudSearch

Introduction

In the previous chapter, we discussed the various best practices that one should follow in order to make the most of DynamoDB's features. In this chapter, we will focus on how to integrate DynamoDB with other AWS services so that we can have our complete application stack in one place itself. Here, we will also explore various data import and export techniques, which can be used easily.

Importing data from AWS S3 to DynamoDB using AWS Data Pipeline

In this recipe, we will see how to import data from AWS S3 and insert it into the DynamoDB table using AWS Data Pipeline. AWS Data Pipeline helps us create various workflows that can be used to manage the data flow between various AWS services. You can read more about AWS pipeline at `https://aws.amazon.com/datapipeline/`.

Getting ready

To get started with this recipe, you should know how to use the DynamoDB console. Also, you should have created a table called `productTable`, and you should also have an AWS S3 bucket containing the data to be imported to DynamoDB. The data needs to be in a special format so that the process should be able to identify the attributes and its data types easily. Here is the sample data:

```
features{"m":{"screen":
{"s":"4.7\" LED-backlit IPS LCD Multi-Touchscreen Shatter proof
glass"},
"camera":{"s":"8MP"},"intMem":{"s":"128GB"},
"processor":{"s":"Dual-Core 1.4 GHz Cyclone (ARM v8-based)"}}}
id{"s":"2"}
price{"n":"1000"}stock{"n":"100"}type{"s":"phone"}mnfr{"s":"Apple"}
name
{"s":"Apple iPhone 6, Gold, 128 GB"}
features{"m":{"author":{"sS":["Prabhakaran Kuppusamy","Uchit
Vyas"]},"ISBN":
{"s":" 978-1783551897"},"dimensions":{"s":"7.5 x 0.5 x 9.2
inches"},"paperback":
{"s":"180 Pages"}}}id{"s":"1"}price{"n":"44.99"}stock{"n":"10"}
type{"s":"book"}
mnfr{"s":"PacktPub"}name{"s":"DynamoDB Applied Design Patterns"}
```

Note that the `control-character delimited` text file uses the **Start of Text (STX/ASCII 02)** and **End of Text (ETX/ASCII 03)** characters to indicate the beginning and end of the data fields or columns respectively. A single line feed (LF/ASCII 10) indicates the end of records.

How to do it...

Let's start with creating a pipeline that accepts the details, which can be used anytime we want to import data to DynamoDB:

1. Go to the AWS Data Pipeline console (`https://console.aws.amazon.com/datapipeline/`).

2. Click on the **Create Pipeline** button. Enter the details in the form, as shown in the following screenshot. Here, we will add details, such as the pipeline name, description, source S3 folder, target DynamoDB table, and so on. We will select a built-in template to import data to DynamoDB:

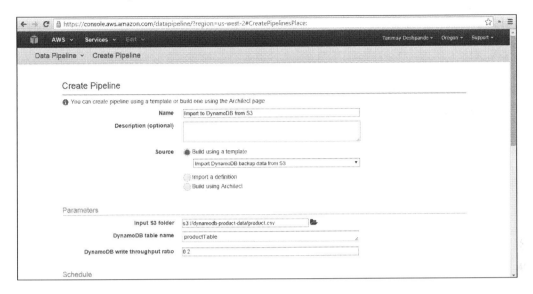

3. Here, we will create a pipeline, which will run only once when it is active. You can also schedule jobs if you need to do this work periodically. You may or may not activate the logging of a pipeline. Note that to create a pipeline using DynamoDB, S3, and EMR, the user or role should have access to these resources. If you have logged in with the root user of the AWS account, then the role will have access to these resources by default:

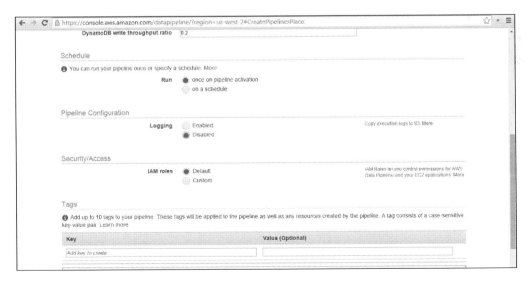

4. Once you click on the **Activate pipeline**, the pipeline will get created, and it will start creating the required resources. Meanwhile, you can keep track of the various activities of the pipeline from the **List Pipeline** page:

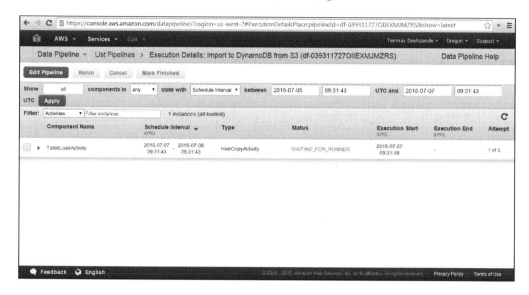

5. This pipeline first creates an EMR cluster, and then uses it to import the data into the DynamoDB table from S3. You can go to the EMR console to see the latest progress. Generally, it takes 5-10 minutes for the EMR cluster to be up and running:

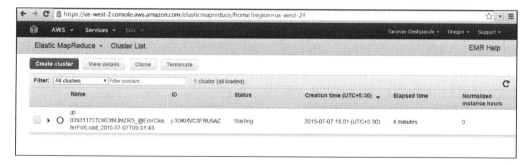

6. Once the EMR cluster is running, the pipeline import will start.

On completion, you will see the data in the DynamoDB table:

How it works...

AWS Data Pipeline is a very helpful tool if you need to move your application data in AWS services. It allows you to easily create the workflow and also decide when to execute it. During the data import from S3, the pipeline first creates the EMR cluster with the default configuration. Once the cluster is running, it uses Hive or Hadoop to first import data from S3 to EMR and writes them to DynamoDB.

As the data pipeline uses the EMR cluster for data import, AWS charges you separately for this. So, before you perform this recipe, you should check the billing for their respective services. Here are some links for the same:

http://aws.amazon.com/datapipeline/pricing/

http://aws.amazon.com/elasticmapreduce/pricing/

http://aws.amazon.com/s3/pricing/

Exporting data from AWS S3 to DynamoDB using AWS Data Pipeline

In this recipe, we will see how to export data from the DynamoDB table to S3 using the AWS Pipeline.

Getting ready

To get started, you need to have a table created and add a few entries to it.

How to do it...

Let's start with creating a pipeline that accepts the details, which can be used anytime we want to execute the export operation:

1. Go to the AWS Data Pipeline console (`https://console.aws.amazon.com/datapipeline/`).

2. Click on the **Create Pipeline** button. Enter the details of the data pipeline configurations in the form, as shown in the following screenshot. Here, we will add details, such as the pipeline `name`, `description`, `source` DynamoDB table name, target `S3` folder, and so on. We select a built-in template to export the DynamoDB data to `S3`:

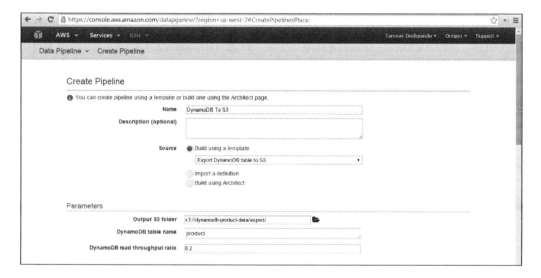

3. Next, we need to provide the details of enabling the logging. Here, we need to provide the `S3` folder location so that if there are any errors and issues, we should be able to debug them from the logs. Now, click on the **Activate** pipeline button. On validation, the AWS Pipeline starts its execution:

4. As part of the execution, the first step is to create the EMR cluster. So, on your screen, you will see the pipeline in `WAITING_FOR_RUNNER` status:

5. Meanwhile, you can also go to the EMR console and see the progress over there.

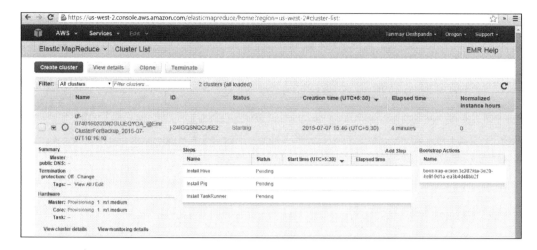

6. Generally, it takes 5-10 minutes for the EMR cluster to get up and running. Once the cluster is up, the pipeline executes the start and is completed if there are no issues:

7. Now you can go to the S3 folder, which you had given as a target folder while creating the pipeline, and see the exported data from DynamoDB. You can download this data on the local machine and see the records.

Here is a screenshot of the exported data:

```
1  features■■{"m":{"screen":{"s":"4.7\" LED-backlit IPS LCD Multi-Touchscreen Shatter proof
   glass"},"camera":{"s":"8MP"},"intMem":{"s":"128GB"},"processor":{"s":"Dual-Core 1.4 GHz Cyclone (ARM
   v8-based)"}}}■■id■■{"s":"2"}■■price■■{"n":"1000"}■■stock■■{"n":"100"}■■type■■{"s":"phone"}■■mnfr■■{
   "s":"Apple"}■■name■■{"s":"Apple iPhone 6, Gold, 128 GB"}
2  features■■{"m":{"author":{"sS":["Prabhakaran Kuppusamy","Uchit Vyas"]},"ISBN":{"s":"
   978-1783551897"},"dimensions":{"s":"7.5 x 0.5 x 9.2 inches"},"paperback":{"s":"180
   Pages"}}}■■id■■{"s":"1"}■■price■■{"n":"44.99"}■■stock■■{"n":"10"}■■type■■{"s":"book"}■■mnfr■■{"s":"
   PacktPub"}■■name■■{"s":"DynamoDB Applied Design Patterns"}
3  features■■{"m":{"screen":{"s":"4.7\" LED-backlit IPS LCD Multi-Touchscreen Shatter proof
   glass"},"camera":{"s":"8MP"},"intMem":{"s":"64GB"},"processor":{"s":"Dual-Core 1.4 GHz Cyclone (ARM
   v8-based)"}}}■■id■■{"s":"1"}■■price■■{"n":"850"}■■stock■■{"n":"120"}■■type■■{"s":"phone"}■■mnfr■■{"
   s":"Apple"}■■name■■{"s":"Apple iPhone 6, Gold, 64 GB"}
4  features■■{"m":{"author":{"s":"Tanmay Deshpande"},"ISBN":{"s":"978-1783551958"},"dimensions":{"s":"7.5 x 0.5
   x 9.2 inches"},"paperback":{"s":"230
   Pages"}}}■■id■■{"s":"5"}■■price■■{"n":"44"}■■stock■■{"n":"20"}■■type■■{"s":"book"}■■mnfr■■{"s":"Pac
   ktPub"}■■name■■{"s":"Mastering DynamoDB"}
5  features■■{"m":{"screen":{"s":"Super AMOLED capacitive
   touchscreen"},"camera":{"s":"8MP"},"intMem":{"s":"64GB"},"processor":{"s":"Quad-core 1.5 GHz Cortex-A53 &
   Quad-core 2.1 GHz - Exynos
   7420"}}}■■id■■{"s":"4"}■■price■■{"n":"820"}■■stock■■{"n":"20"}■■type■■{"s":"phone"}■■mnfr■■{"s":"Sa
   msung"}■■name■■{"s":"Samsung Galaxy S5"}
6  features■■{"m":{"screen":{"s":"Super AMOLED capacitive
   touchscreen"},"camera":{"s":"13MP"},"intMem":{"s":"64GB"},"processor":{"s":"Quad-core 1.5 GHz Cortex-A53 &
   Quad-core 2.1 GHz - Exynos
   7420"}}}■■id■■{"s":"3"}■■price■■{"n":"1119"}■■stock■■{"n":"30"}■■type■■{"s":"phone"}■■mnfr■■{"s":"S
   amsung"}■■name■■{"s":"Samsung Galaxy S6"}
7
```

How it works...

As discussed in the earlier recipe, export also creates the EMR cluster. First, it fetches the data from DynamoDB, and then writes to S3 using Hive or Hadoop. Hadoop itself has a built-in scalability, which makes the overall processes scalable.

As the data pipeline uses the EMR cluster for data import, AWS charges you separately for this. So, before you perform this recipe, you should check the billing for their respective services. It's always a good practice to make sure that the pipeline and the EMR cluster is terminated as soon as your work is done in order to avoid any unnecessary billing.

Accessing the DynamoDB data using AWS EMR

AWS **Elastic MapReduce** (**EMR**) has hosted Hadoop as a service from Amazon. As Hadoop has become one of the most important ETL/analytics tools these days, it is very important to know how to access the DynamoDB data from EMR so that we can use it for analytics. In this recipe, we are going to see how to access the DynamoDB data from EMR for analytics/querying.

Getting ready

To get started, you need to have a DynamoDB table created, and you should have data in it. Also, you need to have a secret key created, which will be used to connect to the EMR cluster using Putty or `ssh` on the UNIX system. In case you haven't, read the documentation at `http://docs.aws.amazon.com/amazondynamodb/latest/developerguide/EMR_SetUp_KeyPair.html`.

This generated .pem `key` can be converted into a private key (`.ppk`), which can be used in Putty. You can refer to the following docs:

- `http://docs.aws.amazon.com/AWSEC2/latest/UserGuide/putty.html`
- `http://docs.aws.amazon.com/AWSEC2/latest/UserGuide/AccessingInstances.html`

How to do it...

Let's get started with access to the DynamoDB data:

1. To get started, we first need to launch the AWS EMR cluster. Go to the EMR console at `https://console.aws.amazon.com/elasticmapreduce/`.

2. You can click on the **Create Cluster** button, and on the next screen, you will see a form asking you for the details of the cluster. You can mention the cluster name and the `S3` folder where the logs need to be stored:

3. Next, you need to specify the Hadoop version. Services, such as Hive/Pig and so on, and hardware configurations need to be installed for your cluster. You also need to mention the number of nodes that you will need in a cluster. In the **Security** and **Access** tab, don't forget to select the key that you created earlier:

4. You can take a look at the other details; once done, you can click on the **Create Cluster** button, which will start the process to create the EMR cluster with a given configuration. Generally, it takes 5-10 minutes for the cluster to be up and running. Once the cluster is up and running, you can connect to the public DNS of the master node and perform the next steps using Putty or any other SSH utility.

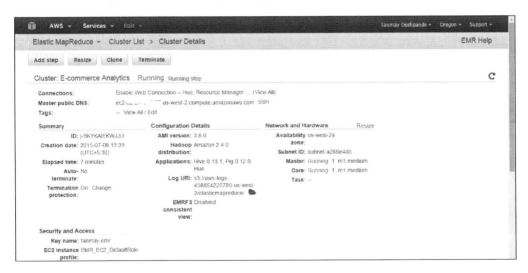

5. Once you connect to the master node, you can type the `hive` command to enter the `hive` prompt. Now, we will create a Hive table, which will map the DynamoDB table details, as shown in the following code snippet:

```
CREATE EXTERNAL TABLE productHiveTable ( // Hive table name

id string, type string, mnfr string, name string,

price bigint, stock bigint)

STORED BY 'org.apache.hadoop.hive.dynamodb.DynamoDBStorageHandler'

TBLPROPERTIES ("dynamodb.table.name" = "product", // DynamoDB
table name

"dynamodb.column.mapping" = "id:id,type:type,  // Mapping of hive
table to

mnfr:mnfr,name:name,price:price,stock:stock");// DynamoDB column
```

The output of the following code snippet is:

```
hadoop@ip-172-31-46-28:~
hive> CREATE EXTERNAL TABLE productHiveTable (
    > id string, type string, mnfr string, name string,
    > price bigint, stock bigint)
    > STORED BY 'org.apache.hadoop.hive.dynamodb.DynamoDBStorageHandler'
    > TBLPROPERTIES ("dynamodb.table.name" = "product",
    > "dynamodb.column.mapping" = "id:id,type:type,mnfr:mnfr,name:name,price:price,stock:stock");
OK
Time taken: 2.175 seconds
hive>
```

6. Now, you can execute a simple select query to see whether the access is working:

```
SELECT * FROM productHiveTable;
```

The output of the following code snippet is:

```
hadoop@ip-172-31-46-28:~
hive> select * from productHiveTable;
OK
2       phone   Apple   Apple iPhone 6, Gold, 128 GB    1000    100
1       phone   Apple   Apple iPhone 6, Gold, 64 GB     850     120
5       book    PacktPub        Mastering DynamoDB      44      20
4       phone   Samsung Samsung Galaxy S5       820     20
3       phone   Samsung Samsung Galaxy S6       1119    30
Time taken: 0.153 seconds, Fetched: 5 row(s)
hive>
```

How it works...

Amazon has developed libraries that help us access the DynamoDB data from EMR. Here, if you take a look at the Hive table creation query, you will notice that we use the `org.apache.hadoop.hive.dynamodb.DynamoDBStorageHandler` class, which helps us map the Hive table with the DynamoDB table data. Every time we invoke any query, EMR connects to DynamoDB, and then fetches/processes the data. While creating the Hive table, we need to carefully map the attributes in the DynamoDB table with proper data types. Amazon supports the following data types of Hive and DynamoDB mapping:

Hive Type	DynamoDB Type
String	String (S)
Bigint or Double	Number (N)
Binary	Binary(B)
Array	Number set (NS), string set (SS), Binary Set (BS)

We need to keep one thing in mind - every time you access this table, EMR will be using the provisioned throughput of that DynamoDB table. So, make sure that while executing the bulk data, it does not consume the provisioned throughput of any other applications. We can control the Hive provisioned throughput rate by setting various variables. For example, you can set `dynamodb.throughput.read.percent` and `dynamodb.throughput.write.percent` to control the read and write capacity units. The value ranges from `0.5` to `1.5`, where `0.5` is the default value, which means Hive will try to use half of the provisioned throughput.

To set the variable, you can call the following command on the Hive prompt:

```
SET dynamodb.throughput.read.percent=1.0;
```

These settings are only valid for a single Hive session, so as soon as you close the Hive prompt, the setting will be ineffective.

Querying the DynamoDB data using AWS EMR

In the previous recipe, we have seen how to access the DynamoDB data from AWS EMR. In this recipe, we are going to see how to query DynamoDB using AWS EMR.

Getting ready

To perform this recipe, you should have performed the earlier recipe and have your EMR cluster still running.

How to do it...

Here, we will use `productHiveTable`, which we created in the previous recipe. In this recipe, we will see how easy it is to query the DynamoDB data using EMR:

1. To get started, connect to your EMR cluster and start Hive.

2. In our e-commerce application, we would like to query the product catalogue data in various ways. With DynamoDB being a NoSQL database, we can only query on hash or range keys themselves, which sometimes makes querying difficult. Now, we can use Hive to effectively query the DynamoDB data.

3. Let's start with our first query to count the total number of products in our DynamoDB table. For this, we need to execute the following query:

   ```
   hive> select count(*) from productHiveTable;
   ```

   This will start a MapReduce job on the EMR cluster, and finally, we will get a count of the total number of products, as shown in the following screenshot:

4. Next, if we want to get all the products manufactured by Apple, and whose cost is less than $1000, we can write the following query:

   ```
   hive> select * from productHiveTable where mnfr="Apple" AND price
   < 1000;
   ```

The output of the following code snippet is:

```
hadoop@ip-172-31-46-28:~
hive> select * from productHiveTable where mnfr="Apple" AND price < 1000;
Total jobs = 1
Launching Job 1 out of 1
Number of reduce tasks is set to 0 since there's no reduce operator
Starting Job = job_1436343305991_0002, Tracking URL = http://172.31.46.28:9046/proxy/application_1436343305991_0002/
Kill Command = /home/hadoop/bin/hadoop job  -kill job_1436343305991_0002
Hadoop job information for Stage-1: number of mappers: 1; number of reducers: 0
2015-07-08 08:28:49,846 Stage-1 map = 0%,  reduce = 0%
2015-07-08 08:29:10,092 Stage-1 map = 100%,  reduce = 0%, Cumulative CPU 5.44 sec
MapReduce Total cumulative CPU time: 5 seconds 440 msec
Ended Job = job_1436343305991_0002
MapReduce Jobs Launched:
Job 0: Map: 1   Cumulative CPU: 5.44 sec   HDFS Read: 289 HDFS Write: 50 SUCCESS
Total MapReduce CPU Time Spent: 5 seconds 440 msec
OK
1       phone   Apple   Apple iPhone 6, Gold, 64 GB       850       120
Time taken: 38.263 seconds, Fetched: 1 row(s)
hive>
```

5. Another query that we can execute is to get the number of products per manufacturer; in this case, we need to execute the following query:

```
hive> select mnfr, count(*) from productHiveTable group by mnfr;
```

The output of the following code is:

```
hadoop@ip-172-31-46-28:~
hive> select mnfr, count(*) from productHiveTable group by mnfr;
Total jobs = 1
Launching Job 1 out of 1
Number of reduce tasks not specified. Estimated from input data size: 1
In order to change the average load for a reducer (in bytes):
  set hive.exec.reducers.bytes.per.reducer=<number>
In order to limit the maximum number of reducers:
  set hive.exec.reducers.max=<number>
In order to set a constant number of reducers:
  set mapreduce.job.reduces=<number>
Starting Job = job_1436343305991_0003, Tracking URL = http://172.31.46.28:9046/proxy/application_1436343305991_0003/
Kill Command = /home/hadoop/bin/hadoop job  -kill job_1436343305991_0003
Hadoop job information for Stage-1: number of mappers: 1; number of reducers: 1
2015-07-08 08:30:48,435 Stage-1 map = 0%,  reduce = 0%
2015-07-08 08:31:07,752 Stage-1 map = 100%,  reduce = 0%, Cumulative CPU 4.42 sec
2015-07-08 08:31:22,648 Stage-1 map = 100%,  reduce = 100%, Cumulative CPU 6.68 sec
MapReduce Total cumulative CPU time: 6 seconds 680 msec
Ended Job = job_1436343305991_0003
MapReduce Jobs Launched:
Job 0: Map: 1 Reduce: 1   Cumulative CPU: 6.68 sec   HDFS Read: 289 HDFS Write: 29 SUCCESS
Total MapReduce CPU Time Spent: 6 seconds 680 msec
OK
Apple   2
PacktPub        1
Samsung 2
Time taken: 56.443 seconds, Fetched: 3 row(s)
hive>
```

6. Similarly, you can execute more such queries in order to get the appropriate information.

How it works...

Every time we use `productHiveTable`, it is going to first fetch the data from DynamoDB and perform the given operation after that. Hive achieves scalability by internally utilizing MapReduce under the hood. For every query, Hive operations will use the provisioned throughput capacity of the DynamoDB table. If you want to avoid this, we can simply import DynamoDB to EMR by performing the following operation:

```
hive> create table productEMR as
    > select * from productHiveTable;
```

The output of the following code:

This will create a new table called `productEMR` and will copy the DynamoDB table data to this table. Now, when we query this table, EMR will not contact DynamoDB. This way, we can effectively create reports on the DynamoDB data.

Performing join operations on the DynamoDB data using AWS EMR

In the previous recipe, we saw how to use EMR to access the DynamoDB data and query the same as well. In this recipe, we will see how to join two DynamoDB tables in order to get the combined view.

Getting ready

To perform this recipe, you should have performed the earlier recipe and should have your EMR cluster still running.

How to do it...

Here, we will use two tables: one is the `Customer` table, and the other one is the `Orders` table. The `Customer` table contains detailed information of the customer, while the `Order` table contains the details of the order, along with `customerId`, which provides a link between these two tables. Now we want to execute queries that need information from both tables, which cannot be achieved solely by DynamoDB, and so, we use EMR:

1. To get started, we need to make sure that we have two tables created, as mentioned earlier. Now, we will connect to the EMR cluster, and we will create two Hive tables corresponding to these tables in DynamoDB, as shown in the following code snippet:

```
CREATE EXTERNAL TABLE customerHiveTable (
   id string, fname string, lname string,
   city string, state string, country  string)
   STORED BY
   'org.apache.hadoop.hive.dynamodb.DynamoDBStorageHandler'
     TBLPROPERTIES ("dynamodb.table.name" = "customer",
     "dynamodb.column.mapping" =
     "id:id,fname:fname,lname:lname,city:city,
     state:state,country:country");
CREATE EXTERNAL TABLE ordersHiveTable (
   orderId string, customerId string, productId string,
     orderedDate string, currentStatus string)
   STORED BY
   'org.apache.hadoop.hive.dynamodb.DynamoDBStorageHandler'
     TBLPROPERTIES ("dynamodb.table.name" = "orders",
     "dynamodb.column.mapping" = "orderId:orderId,
     customerId:customerId,productId:productId,
     orderedDate:orderedDate,currentStatus:currentStatus");
```

2. Now, in order to confirm that the Hive tables are able to fetch data from DynamoDB, we can execute the SELECT queries and see whether we are able to see the data:

```
SELECT * from customerHiveTable;
SELECT * from ordersHiveTable;
```

Next we can build up any query which needs information from both tables and get data as required. For example, consider we need to know the names of customer and current status of their orders then we can execute following query.SELECT c.fname, c.lname, o.orderedDate, o.currentStatus FROM
ordersHiveTable o JOIN customerHiveTable c
ON (o.customerId = c.id);

3. In the previous recipe, we created a product table. Now, we can also use this table to join with the orders table in order to get a clearer view:

```
SELECT p.name, o.orderedDate, o.currentStatus FROM
ordersHiveTable o JOIN productHiveTable p
ON ( o.productId = p.id);
```

How it works...

As explained in the earlier recipe, DynamoDBStorageHandler helps EMR connect to DynamoDB. As EMR/Hive keeps on reading the data, MapReduce jobs get executed in order and get the desired output. You can also create an internal Hive table, and first fetch the complete DynamoDB table data into it, and later, perform the join queries on the Hive table.

Exporting data to AWS S3 from DynamoDB using AWS EMR

In the first recipe of this chapter, we saw how to use the AWS Pipeline to export the DynamoDB data to S3. The AWS Pipeline creation and execution is easy and quick, but we have very little control on things that happen in the pipeline, so we now are going to talk about one recipe that will explain how to export the DynamoDB data to S3 using EMR.

Getting ready

To perform this recipe, you should have performed the earlier recipe and have your EMR cluster still running.

How to do it...

Let's export data to AWS S3 from DynamoDB:

1. To perform this recipe, we need to create two tables. In the earlier recipes, we have already created `productHiveTable`, as shown in the following code:

```
CREATE EXTERNAL TABLE productHiveTable (
id string, type string, mnfr string, name string,
price bigint, stock bigint)
STORED BY 'org.apache.hadoop.hive.dynamodb.DynamoDBStorageHandler'
TBLPROPERTIES ("dynamodb.table.name" = "product",
"dynamodb.column.mapping" = "id:id,type:type,mnfr:mnfr,
name:name,price:price,stock:stock");
```

2. We need to create one more external table in Hive that directs to the S3 folder path, where we need to export our data:

```
CREATE EXTERNAL TABLE productS3Table (
id string, type string, mnfr string, name string,
price bigint, stock bigint)
ROW FORMAT DELIMITED FIELDS TERMINATED BY '|'
LOCATION 's3://myawsbucket/product/';
```

In the location, we need to specify the bucket name and folder name where the data should be exported.

3. Now, we need to execute the following query to start the data export process:

```
INSERT OVERWRITE TABLE productS3Table
SELECT * FROM productHiveTable;
```

4. Once the MapReduce job is complete, you can go and check your S3 bucket. You should be able to see your data in a text file with attributes, which are pipe separated.

How it works...

EMR first fetches the data from the DynamoDB table and starts writing it to the S3 bucket location. Using this method for data export, we get a better control on how the data should be formatted. We can also export selective data by providing conditions to the select query. For instance, if we want to export only those products that are manufactured by Apple, then we can do this by executing the following query:

```
INSERT OVERWRITE TABLE productS3Table
SELECT * FROM productHiveTable WHERE mnfr="Apple";
```

Make a note of the preceding statement, as this would overwrite the existing data in the given S3 folder.

Logging DynamoDB operations using AWS CloudTrail

This is a very simple recipe that helps us enable the logging of any DynamoDB operations using CloudTrail. CloudTrail is a global logging service by AWS, which allows us to create logs of all the events that happened on scribed services. It creates JSON documents for every operation that occurs and saves it in the provided S3 bucket.

Getting ready

To perform this recipe, you need to know how to use the DynamoDB console.

How to do it...

Let's log into DynamoDB by using AWS CloudTrail:

1. To keep track of events happening in various AWS services, we need to first enable logging of the **CloudTrail** events. To do so, first login to the AWS CloudTrail console, which is available at: `https://console.aws.amazon.com/cloudtrail`.

2. We enable the **CloudTrail** logs and also provide the S3 bucket location, where we would like to see the event to be saved:

3. By clicking on the **Advanced link**, you can also enable publishing the availability of the **CloudTrail** events in the S3 bucket, if you don't want to keep looking for events in S3 forever.

4. Now, if you go to the DynamoDB console and create a new table, you will see the corresponding event for the same in the S3 location. Here is how a sample `CreateTable` event looks:

```
{
    "eventVersion": "1.03",
    "userIdentity": {
      "type": "Root",
      "principalId": "458854225780",
      "arn": "arn:aws:iam::458854225780:root",
      "accountId": "123494959950",
      "accessKeyId": "ABSCLLFNKFKKFLF",
        "sessionContext": {
        "attributes": {
          "mfaAuthenticated": "false",
          "creationDate": "2015-07-09T08:41:22Z"
      }
      }
      },
    "eventTime": "2015-07-09T09:48:07Z",
    "eventSource": "dynamodb.amazonaws.com",
    "eventName": "CreateTable",
    "awsRegion": "us-west-2",
    "sourceIPAddress": "199.43.186.25",
    "userAgent": "console.amazonaws.com",
    "requestParameters": {
      "provisionedThroughput": {
        "writeCapacityUnits": 1,
        "readCapacityUnits": 1
      },
```

```
        "tableName": "customer",
      "keySchema": [{
        "attributeName": "id",
          "keyType": "HASH"
      }],
      "attributeDefinitions": [{
        "attributeType": "S",
          "attributeName": "id"
        }]
      }
```

How it works...

The CloudTrail logs provide detailed information about when the event occurred, the user name, and event details in depth. This kind of information is helpful when something goes wrong and you need to track what happened. There is no additional cost for enabling the CloudTrail event service (see `http://aws.amazon.com/cloudtrail/pricing/` for further details), but we need to pay for the S3 storage to store these events.

Exporting the DynamoDB data to AWS Redshift

AWS provides the petabyte-scale data warehouse as a service in Cloud. It provides us with SQL-like tools to perform business intelligence on virtually any size data. It is quite natural to we use DynamoDB as our application database. We would need to use the data warehouse tools to do analytics. So, in this recipe, we will see how to launch the Redshift cluster and import the DynamoDB data to it.

Getting ready

To perform this recipe, you need to know how to use the DynamoDB console. Also, follow the instructions to install the prerequisites for AWS Redshift from `http://docs.aws.amazon.com/redshift/latest/gsg/rs-gsg-prereq.html`.

How to do it...

To get started, we will first see how to launch the Redshift cluster, and then use the `COPY` command to import the DynamoDB data into it:

1. Go to the AWS Redshift console (`https://console.aws.amazon.com/redshift/`):

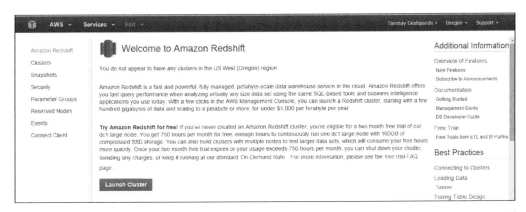

2. Click on the **Launch Cluster** button. On the next screen, you will need to enter the details for the cluster, for example, the cluster name, username, password, port, and so on:

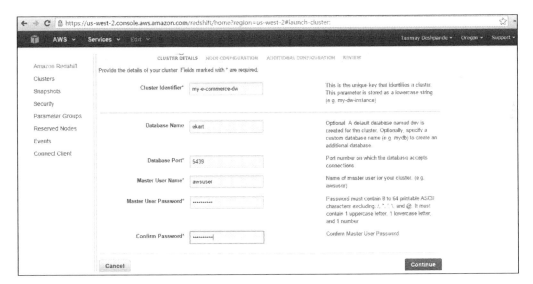

3. Next, you will need to select the hardware configuration, and click on the **Continue** button:

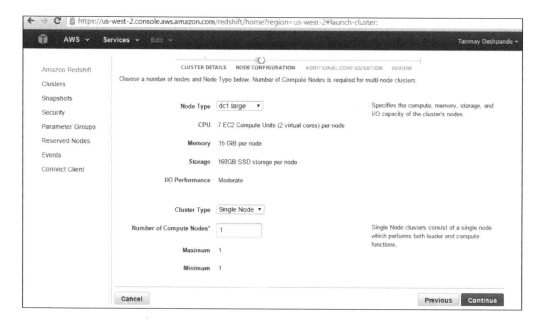

4. After this, you will need to select the security configurations for your **Amazon Redshift** cluster. Note that the security group you select should have an inbound rule to allow traffic from your machine to the Redshift cluster:

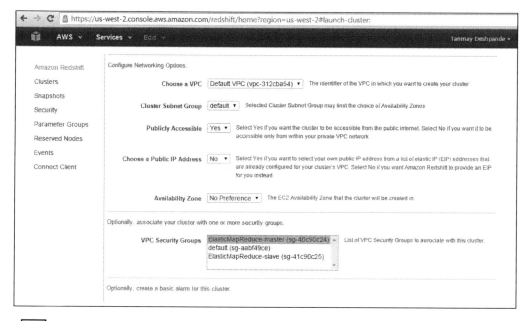

5. Review the cluster settings, and click on the **Launch Cluster** button.

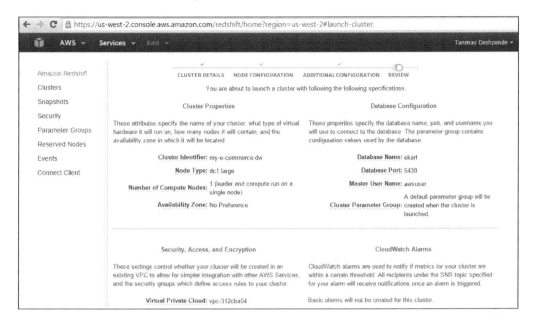

6. Next, you can start the SQL workbench and connect to Redshift using the provided JDBC URL on your AWS Redshift console. Once the connection is successful, we first need to create a table in Redshift in which we will import the DynamoDB data. Here is the syntax to do this:

```
create table productDW(
id varchar(20), type varchar(20), mnfr varchar(20), name
varchar(50),
price int, stock int);
```

On successful validations, you will see the following table getting created:

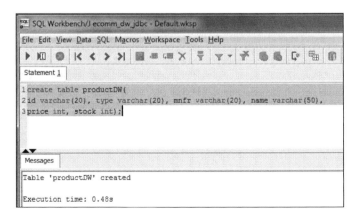

7. Next, we have to use the COPY command provided by AWS to import data to the newly created table:

```
copy productDW from 'dynamodb://product'
credentials 'aws_access_key_id=<your-aws-access-key>;aws_secret_
access_key=<your-aws-secret-key>'
readratio 50;
```

Here, we need to specify the names of the source and target table properly. This command expects the Redshift and DynamoDB tables to be in the same AWS region. We also need to provide one parameter, that is, retardation. This parameter is used to define how much of provisioned read capacity units the COPY command needs to use in order to fetch the data from DynamoDB. We have set this parameter to 50, which means that the COPY command will use 50 percent of the provisioned throughput for this operation:

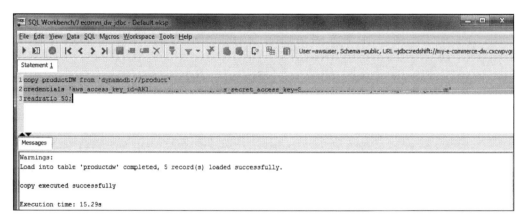

8. Once the load is complete, you can check whether the records are imported properly by executing the select * command:

```
select * from productDW;
```

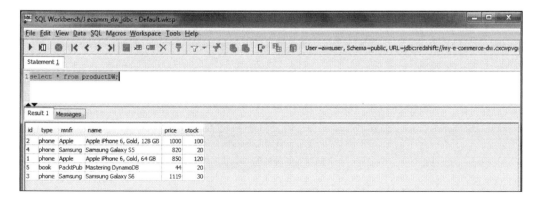

9. Now, you are free to execute any queries and perform analytics on this data to get more information about the data we have.

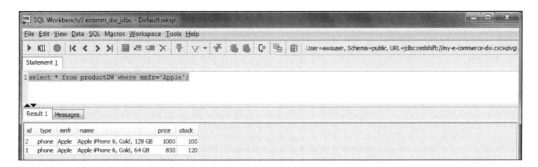

How it works...

The COPY command simply does what its name suggests. The only thing that we need to ensure is that the Redshift cluster and DynamoDB table have to be in the same AWS region. Here, the data types of DynamoDB and Redshift are different, so while designing the table, we need to give special attention to them. Unlike the EMR external table, the COPY command fetches the DynamoDB data only once in Redshift; so once the data load is done, we don't need to bother about Redshift consuming the DynamoDB throughput.

Before we start with the recipe, make sure that you are aware of the Redshift pricing. You may also take advantage of the Redshift free tier from `http://aws.amazon.com/redshift/pricing/`.

Importing the DynamoDB data to AWS CloudSearch

AWS CloudSearch is a search engine in AWS that allows us to perform full text searches on the documents uploaded. Many times, this functionality is helpful, as you only query hash and range keys in DynamoDB for exact searches. In this recipe, we are going to see how to integrate DynamoDB with CloudSearch so that we can search data more effectively.

Getting ready

To perform this recipe, you need to know how to use the AWS console.

How to do it...

To get started, we will first see how to launch the CloudSearch domain and import the DynamoDB table to it:

1. Go to the AWS CloudSearch console (`http://console.aws.amazon.com/cloudsearch/`).

2. Click on the **Create New Domain button**, which will prompt you fill in a form to include details. Here, you need to specify the domain name, number of instances, and instance types:

3. On the next screen, you need to choose where to import the data from. Here, select **Analyze sample item(s) from Amazon DynamoDB**. I also need to select the table to be imported, read capacity, and hash and range keys from where we need to import the data:

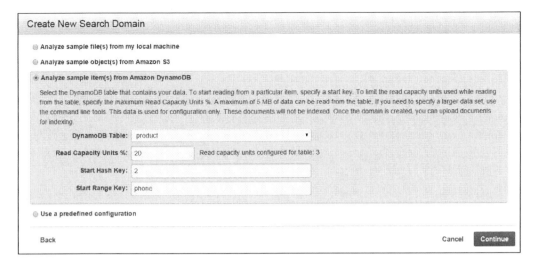

4. On providing the proper inputs, it will automatically fetch the attribute types and suggest the indexing options. Here, you can keep the default settings or choose to change the settings if required:

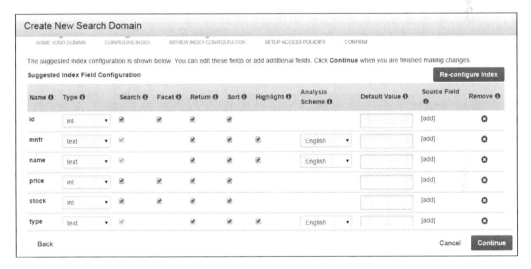

5. On the next screen, you will need to choose the security policy for the cluster access. You can choose the required one as per your need:

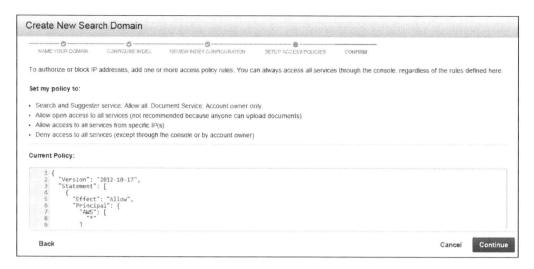

6. On the next screen, it will display the details to be confirmed. After a review, you can click on the **Confirm** button, which starts the launch of the cluster. Generally, this takes 5-10 minutes to get your domain up and running.

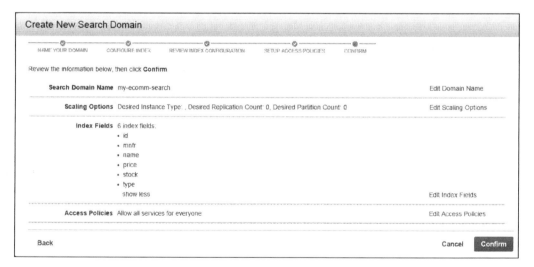

7. On a successful launch, you will see that all the DynamoDB documents get imported to the CloudSearch domain.

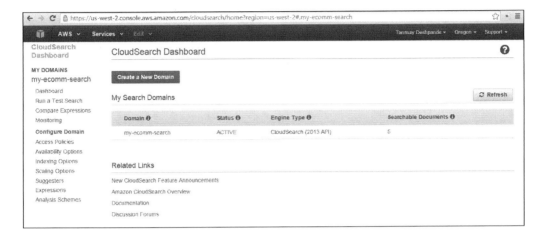

How it works...

This import of documents is a one time activity only; this sets a sync process between the DynamoDB table and the CloudSearch domain. There are options to keep the DynamoDB data in sync with the CloudSearch domain. The first one creates a new domain every time and loads the complete data from DynamoDB, and the second one is used to programmatically sync the DynamoDB data with the CloudSearch domain. The first option is simple, but, sometimes, it can be costly. The second option will take some of your efforts, but it will be a more reliable way.

Performing a full text search on the DynamoDB data using CloudSearch

In the previous recipe, we saw how to import DynamoDB to CloudSearch. In this recipe, we will see how to perform a full text search on the same data.

Getting ready

To perform this recipe, you should have performed the earlier recipe.

How to do it...

Let's perform a full text search on the DynamoDB:

1. CloudSearch gives us a built-in capability to perform a full text, faceted search. To get started, we need to click on the **Run a Test Search** link:

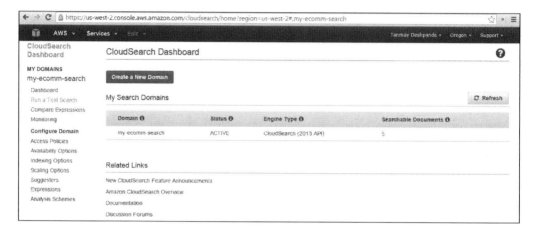

2. On this screen, you will see a textbox where you can type your query, for example, I need to search a query `'Samsung'`; then, I need to type this in the textbox and click on the **Go** button. It will search in documents and return the results.

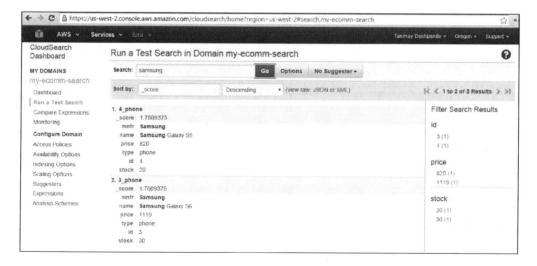

3. You can also perform a search on a specific attribute by expanding the **Options** section on same screen. For example, if I want to search only those products that are manufactured by `PacktPub`, I can do this in the following manner, as shown in the following screenshot:

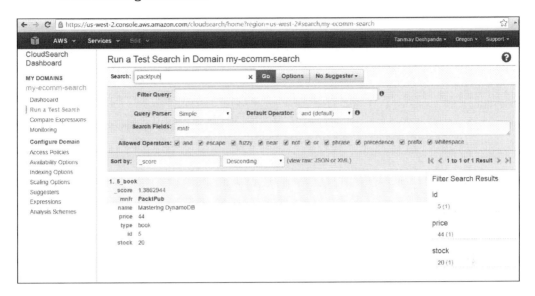

4. You can also use various operators, such as OR, AND, and so on, to perform query operations. Here, you can select the **Lucene** Query parser from the options section and execute the query.

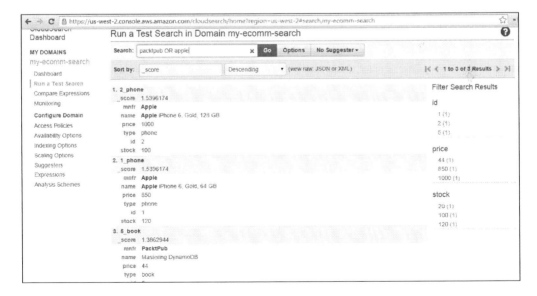

5. You can also use the AWS SDK to perform these searches programmatically in order to integrate with your applications.

How it works...

Here, we are using all built-in features of CloudSearch. Internally, it maintains the indexes and keeps comparing those with the input queries. It also builds a relevance index and returns the results in an ordered manner so that the matching documents are returned first. A faceted search helps us provide a more detailed search for end users.

Note that CloudSearch has its own pricing model. While importing data from DynamoDB, it uses its provisioned throughput, so keep an eye on your usage and the billing.

9
Developing Web Applications using DynamoDB

In this chapter, we will cover the following topics:

> - Performing data modeling and table creations
> - Developing services for the sign-up activity for web applications
> - Developing services for the sign-in activity for web applications
> - Developing services for the Address Book application
> - Deploying web applications on AWS Elastic Beanstalk

Introduction

In the earlier chapters, we learned various things about DynamoDB and worked on various recipes to see how things work. Now, it's time to develop a real-world application step by step, integrating all the pieces together to build an Internet scalable web application.

In this chapter, we are going to see how to build an Address Book web application. The requirements are quite similar to any application that we use these days:

> - A new user should be able to register to the application
> - A registered user should be able to log in to the application
> - A logged-in user should be able to add new contacts
> - A logged-in user should be able to view the already added contacts

We would also like to see our application being hosted on AWS Beanstalk so that any user on the Internet should be able to use this application.

The technology stack for this application would be as follows:

- ▶ Java for backend services
- ▶ Spring MVC for the REST API development
- ▶ DynamoDB for data storage
- ▶ AngularJS for frontend
- ▶ AWS Elastic Beanstalk to deploy and scale the application in Cloud

The complete code for this application can be downloaded from `https://github.com/deshpandetanmay/dynamodb-cookbook`.

Performing data modeling and table creations

In this recipe, we will see how to model data for this web application and create a DynamoDB table accordingly.

Getting ready

To get started with this recipe, you need to know how to create a table in DynamoDB using the console.

How to do it...

To perform data modeling for any web application using the NoSQL database as a backend, we need to first start with what queries we would like to execute on the tables. Considering the requirements, we will need at least two tables:

- ▶ **User**: This is a table used to store information of a valid user's details along with the credentials
- ▶ **Contact**: This is a table used to store information of all the contacts added by the users

As we will use the `user` table to save the registered user's information, as well as to sign-in, we can use `email` as the hash key for this table.

Here, we won't need a range key as the e-mail ID should be good enough to recognize a user for its registration and login. So, let's create the `user` table with `email` as the hash key:

1. Log in to the AWS console and go to DynamoDB at `https://console.aws.amazon.com/dynamodb/`.

2. Create the `user` table by providing the e-mail as the hash key and the data type as String.

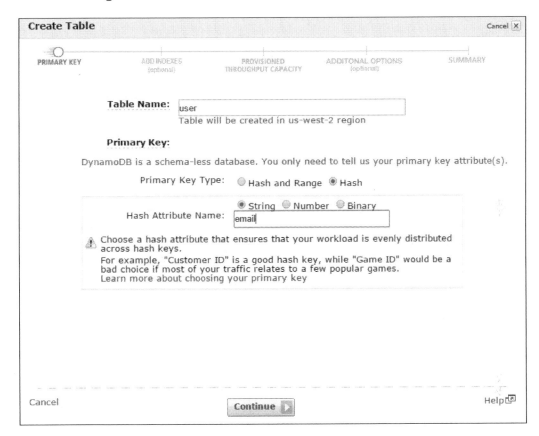

3. Here, we don't need to create any secondary indexes, so we skip to the provisioned throughput page and give some numbers. As we are creating this app for learning purposes, we can set the read and write capacity units to 10 each. Now, proceed to complete the table creation process.

4. Next, we need to create the `contact` table. This table will be used to store contacts for each registered user. So, we can create this table by providing the contact `id` as the hash key and `parentId` as the range key. Here, `parentId` can be the e-mail ID of the user to whom the contact belongs to.

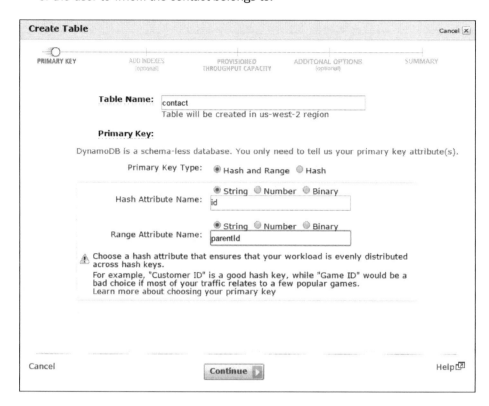

5. Next, we click on **Continue** to proceed. Here, we don't need to create any secondary index, so we skip to the provisioned throughput page. Given that we would be querying this table, as compared to the user table, it's safe to provision a higher read/write throughput. Let's say we give 25 units to each. Proceed and complete the table creation.

How it works...

The strategy behind designing this schema is to provide easy access to register, login, and contact services. Here, we chose an e-mail as the hash key, as we know that each user will have a unique e-mail ID, and this will also allow an even distribution of data among DynamoDB partitions. Also, we can easily fetch the password for a given e-mail ID in order to verify the credentials.

In the contact table, we will have the hash key as the contact ID and the range key as the e-mail ID of a user who added this contact. We don't need to fetch contacts by their IDs, so we will use auto-generated values for this attribute. On the other hand, we would need to fetch all the contacts added by a specific user, which can be supported by the range key.

Developing services for the sign-up activity for web applications

In the earlier recipe, we created DynamoDB tables based on the need. Now, we will write services to put the data into DynamoDB and get the data back for our application. In this recipe, we will learn how to write services for the sign-up/user registration activity.

Getting ready

To get started with this recipe, you need to know to use the AWS SDK for DynamoDB.

How to do it...

Let's write services to put the data into DynamoDB:

1. To get started, we will first create a **maven** project and add the AWS SDK:

   ```
   dependency:<dependency>
     <groupId>com.amazonaws</groupId>
     <artifactId>aws-java-sdk-dynamodb</artifactId>
     <version>1.10.4.1</version>
   </dependency>
   ```

2. Next, we will create a `model` class for the user table. Here, we will use the `DynamoDBMapper` class to connect to DynamoDB using Object Persistence Model. We will also consider attributes, such as the first name, last name, password, and so on for the user registration, apart from our hash key, that is, an e-mail:

   ```
   @DynamoDBTable(tableName = "user")
   public class User {
     private String email;
     private String password;
     private String fname;
     private String lname;
     @DoNotTouch
     @DynamoDBHashKey(attributeName = "email")
     public String getEmail() {
       return email;
   ```

```
    }
    public void setEmail(String email) {
      this.email = email;
    }
    @DynamoDBAttribute(attributeName = "password")
    public String getPassword() {
      return password;
    }
    public void setPassword(String password) {
      this.password = password;
    }
    @DoNotTouch
    @DynamoDBAttribute(attributeName = "fname")
    public String getFname() {
      return fname;
    }
    public void setFname(String fname) {
      this.fname = fname;
    }
    @DoNotTouch
    @DynamoDBAttribute(attributeName = "lname")
    public String getLname() {
      return lname;
    }
    public void setLname(String lname) {
      this.lname = lname;
    }
  }
```

3. Here, we would like to save the user password in an encrypted format, so we are going to use the DynamoDB encryption library (which was already discussed in *Chapter 6, Securing DynamoDB*). So, we also need to include the maven dependency for the same:

```
<dependency>
  <groupId>com.amazonaws</groupId>
  <artifactId>aws-dynamodb-encryption-java</artifactId>
  <version>0.0.3-SNAPSHOT</version>
  <exclusions>
    <exclusion>
      <groupId>com.amazonaws</groupId>
      <artifactId>aws-java-sdk</artifactId>
    </exclusion>
  </exclusions>
</dependency>
```

4. Next, we will write a simple Java code to invoke the `DynamoDBMapper` methods to save and get the user records by an e-mail:

```
// Initiate DynamoDB client providing credentials and
EncryptorProvider class
  static AmazonDynamoDBClient client = new AmazonDynamoDBClient(
  new ClasspathPropertiesFileCredentialsProvider());
  static DynamoDBMapper mapper = new DynamoDBMapper(client,
    DynamoDBMapperConfig.DEFAULT, new AttributeEncryptor(
  EncryptorProvider.getProvider()));
  static {
    client.setRegion(Region.getRegion(Regions.US_WEST_2));
  }
//Create user method
  public void createUser(User user) {
    mapper.save(user);
  }
```

Here, we have mentioned `EncryptorProvider`, so we need to write a class that provides the encryption provider to the `DynamoDBMapper` class. We will use the encryption library provided by AWS.

5. It contains various methods, such as the encryption key generator, signing key generator, and a method to create `EncryptionMaterialsProvider`:

```
static SecureRandom rnd = new SecureRandom();
// generate encryption key
  private static SecretKey generateEncryptionKey() {
    KeyGenerator aesGen = null;
    try {
      aesGen = KeyGenerator.getInstance("AES");
    } catch (NoSuchAlgorithmException e1) {
      e1.printStackTrace();
    }
    aesGen.init(128, rnd);
    return aesGen.generateKey();
  }
  // generate signing key
  private static SecretKey generateSigningKey() {
    KeyGenerator macGen = null;
    try {
      macGen = KeyGenerator.getInstance("HmacSHA256");
    } catch (NoSuchAlgorithmException e) {
      e.printStackTrace();
    }
    macGen.init(256, rnd);
    return macGen.generateKey();
```

```
    }
    //Method to initiate EncryptionMaterialsProvider
    public static EncryptionMaterialsProvider getProvider() {
        SecretKey encKey = null;
        SecretKey signingKey = null;
        encKey = generateEncryptionKey();
        signingKey = generateSigningKey();
        return new SymmetricStaticProvider(encKey, signingKey);
    }
```

6. Next, we need to write a `controller` class, which will invoke our services. Here, I am using Spring MVC so that I can have the web services generated. You can read more about Spring MVC at `http://docs.spring.io/spring/docs/current/spring-framework-reference/html/mvc.html`.

    Here is a code snippet that will invoke the create user service:

```
@Autowired
private UserService userService;
@RequestMapping(value = "/v1/register", method = RequestMethod.
POST,
    consumes = MediaType.APPLICATION_JSON_VALUE)
@ResponseStatus(value = HttpStatus.OK)
public void register(@RequestBody User user) {
    userService.createUser(user);
}
```

7. Now we can build the project and deploy it to the Tomcat webserver to test our service. Here is snippet of how we can test our API using the Postman REST client. You can read more about the Postman rest client at `https://www.getpostman.com/`.

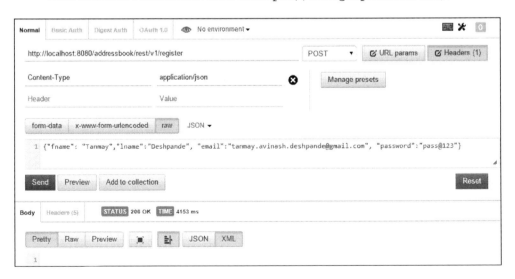

8. Next, we need to build the user interface, which accepts the details from the user and calls our API to save the data to DynamoDB. We will use some popular UI frameworks, such as HTML, AngularJS, and Bootstrap, and so on. Now when we deploy our application again to Tomcat, we can see the registration page. If you want to use anything else apart from the earlier mentioned technologies, you can do so.

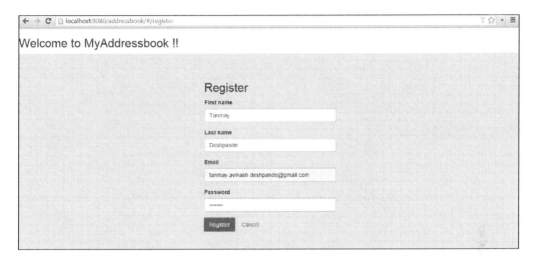

9. On successful registration, you should be able to see the data being saved in DynamoDB table. You will see one record in the user table where the password is encrypted. Here is a snapshot of the user table:

How it works...

Here, we are using the same topics that we learned in the earlier chapters. So, when we invoke the API from UI, it ultimately invokes the corresponding DynamoDB APIs.

Developing services for the sign-in activity for web applications

In the earlier recipe, we wrote and tested services for user registration. In this recipe, we will implement services for the user sign-in.

Getting ready

To get started with this recipe, you should have performed the earlier recipe.

How to do it...

For this recipe, we will use the same project that we created earlier:

1. To start with, we use the same user model that we defined in the earlier recipe. As we had encrypted the password during registration, it is very important to use the same client, which was initiated by the encryption provider:

```
static AmazonDynamoDBClient client = new AmazonDynamoDBClient(
        new ClasspathPropertiesFileCredentialsProvider());
static DynamoDBMapper mapper = new DynamoDBMapper(client,
    DynamoDBMapperConfig.DEFAULT, new AttributeEncryptor(
        EncryptorProvider.getProvider()));
static {
client.setRegion(Region.getRegion(Regions.US_WEST_2));
}
```

2. Next, we write a method which will fetch the user record for a given e-mail ID:

```
public User getUserByEmail(String email) {
        return mapper.load(User.class, email);
}
```

3. Next, we write a `controller` class using Spring MVC components to which we will provide a REST API:

```
@RequestMapping(value = "/v1/login", method = RequestMethod.POST,
consumes = MediaType.APPLICATION_JSON_VALUE)
@ResponseStatus(value = HttpStatus.OK)
public void login(@RequestBody User user) {
User fetchedUser = userService.getUserByEmail(user.getEmail());
    if (fetchedUser.getPassword().equals(user.getPassword())) {
      //return response
```

```
    } else {
        throw new RuntimeException("Invalid email or password");
    }
}
```

Here, we check whether the password provided by the user from the UI page matches with the one that is stored. If it does not, we throw an exception.

4. Now we can build the project and deploy the war to the local Tomcat in order to see whether it is working or not. Again, we will use the Postman REST client to verify our APIs:

5. Next, we write HTML and JavaScript to build the login page, which accepts the e-mail ID and password, and we can integrate the API we tested earlier with the UI. On a successful build, we will, again, deploy the war to the local Tomcat, and we will now see the working model:

6. We click on the **Login** button, and we will be able to log in if we are provided the credentials that match with the stored one in DynamoDB; otherwise, we get an error message:

How it works...

Here, we simply fetch the data of the user and compare the password. As we use the encryption library, the decryption of the password is handled by the same library itself, so we don't need to write anything extra there.

Of course, this is very basic way of authentication. You can also think about using Web Identity Federation APIs in case you want to support sign up/in using social accounts, such as Google, Facebook, and Amazon accounts.

Developing services for the Address Book application

Now that we are done with the sign-up and sign-in activities for our address book application, it's time to get star ted with developing address-related services. In this recipe, we will develop two APIs, one to add a new contact and another one to view all the contacts.

Getting ready

To get started with this recipe, you should have performed the earlier recipe.

How to do it...

For this recipe, we will also use the same project setup that we had earlier:

1. To get started, we need to first create a model class for a contact record in the contact table. Here, we create the table with the hash key as ID (auto-generated) and the range key as the parent ID (e-mail ID of the user who added this contact):

```
@DynamoDBTable(tableName = "contact")
public class Contact {
  private String id;
  private String parentId;
  private String fname;
  private String lname;
  private String phone;
  private String email;
  @DynamoDBHashKey
  @DynamoDBAutoGeneratedKey
  public String getId() {
    return id;
  }
  public void setId(String id) {
    this.id = id;
  }
  @DynamoDBRangeKey
  public String getParentId() {
    return parentId;
  }
  public void setParentId(String parentId) {
    this.parentId = parentId;
  }
  public String getFname() {
    return fname;
  }
  public void setFname(String fname) {
    this.fname = fname;
  }
  public String getLname() {
    return lname;
  }
  public void setLname(String lname) {
    this.lname = lname;
  }
```

```
        public String getPhone() {
          return phone;
        }
        public void setPhone(String phone) {
          this.phone = phone;
        }
        public String getEmail() {
          return email;
        }
        public void setEmail(String email) {
          this.email = email;
        }}
```

2. Next, we will initiate the `DynamoDB client` class and the `DynamoDBMapper` class, which will help us perform various operations on the DynamoDB table:

```
static AmazonDynamoDBClient client = new AmazonDynamoDBClient(
  new ClasspathPropertiesFileCredentialsProvider());
  static {
  client.setRegion(Region.getRegion(Regions.US_WEST_2));
}
DynamoDBMapper mapper = new DynamoDBMapper(client);
```

3. Now, we need to write a service to add a new contact to DynamoDB:

```
public void addContact(Contact contact) {
  mapper.save(contact);
}
```

4. We need to write the corresponding `Controller` method as well so that this service can be integrated with UI:

```
@Autowired
private AddressBookService addressBookService;
@RequestMapping(value = "/v1/contact", method = RequestMethod.
POST,
  consumes = MediaType.APPLICATION_JSON_VALUE)
@ResponseStatus(value = HttpStatus.OK)
public void addContact(@RequestBody Contact contact) {
  addressBookService.addContact(contact);
}
```

5. Now, we can test this API by building and deploying the war file to Tomcat.

6. Let's write a service to get all the contacts of a given user. To do so, we will pass the e-mail ID of the logged in user to the service, and then, the service will return the contacts added by this user:

```java
public List<Contact> getAllContacts(String userEmailId) {
    List<Contact> contactList = new ArrayList<Contact>();
    // Condition to get records for given userEmailId
    Condition condition = new Condition().withComparisonOperator(
        ComparisonOperator.EQ.toString()).withAttributeValueList(
            new AttributeValue().withS(userEmailId));
    DynamoDBScanExpression scanExpression = new
        DynamoDBScanExpression();
    scanExpression.addFilterCondition("parentId", condition);
    // Paginated scan in case no. of contacts are too much
    PaginatedParallelScanList<Contact> contacts = mapper.
parallelScan(
Contact.class, scanExpression, 4);
    for (Contact contact : contacts) {
        contactList.add(contact);
    }
    return contactList;
}
```

7. Next, we write the `controller` method, which will call this service and fetch all the contacts of the given e-mail ID:

```
@RequestMapping(value = "/v1/contact/all", method = RequestMethod.
GET, produces = MediaType.APPLICATION_JSON_VALUE)
@ResponseStatus(value = HttpStatus.OK)
@ResponseBody
public List<Contact> getAllContacts(@RequestParam String
userEmail) {
    return addressBookService.getAllContacts(userEmail);
}
```

8. Next, we build and deploy the service and test it using the Postman REST API.

9. Here, we will see that the entries have been added by my user only. If we try to invoke the API by another e-mail, I would not be able to see someone else's contacts. For example, if I invoke this API by some other e-mail ID, I won't get any contacts back.

10. Now, we will integrate this API with the UI code in order to get the end-to-end application working. First, we will log in to our app by providing the credentials that we created earlier. Once you have logged in, you can see a form that accepts the details to add a new contact.

11. Once we click on the **Add New Contact** button, it will invoke our API to add a new contact to DynamoDB. At the bottom of the page, you will see a list of your contacts:

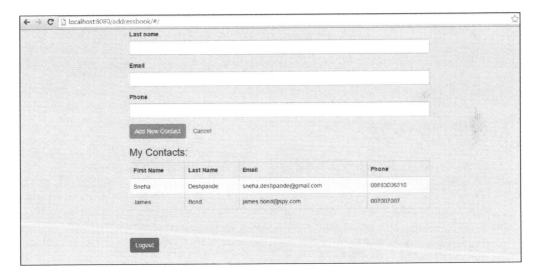

How it works...

Once we invoke the buttons, **Add New Contact** button will call the APIs we have developed. Here, you Address Book application can use any UI framework you are comfortable with. The source code for this application can be downloaded from `https://github.com/deshpandetanmay/dynamodb-cookbook`.

Deploying web applications on AWS Elastic Beanstalk

AWS Elastic Beanstalk allows you to quickly deploy your applications on Cloud, and they can be made accessible to the public. You can build your applications in languages, such as Java, PHP, Ruby, and so on and deploy them to the application server of your choice, such as Apache Tomcat, PHP, Windows Server, Node.js, and so on.

You can read more about Elastic Beanstalk at `http://docs.aws.amazon.com/elasticbeanstalk/latest/dg/Welcome.html`.

In this recipe, we will see how to deploy the Address Book application using Elastic Beanstalk and access it from Cloud.

Getting ready

To get started with this recipe, you should already have built your application and tested it locally. There are several ways to deploy the application, but for this recipe, we will use the Eclipse AWS Toolkit. You should also have installed the AWS Toolkit for Eclipse. If you haven't done this yet, you can refer to `http://docs.aws.amazon.com/AWSToolkitEclipse/latest/GettingStartedGuide/tke_setup_install.html` for more details.

How to do it...

Let's deploy Address Book application using Elastic Beanstalk and access it from Cloud:

1. First of all, if you have downloaded the source code from the dynamodb-cookbook git hub repository for this application, then build the project to create the required jars and war. To do so, go to the address folder and execute the following command:

   `mvn clean install`

```
C:\Users\tanmay_deshpande\git\dynamodb-cookbook\addressbook-elasticbeanstalk\add
ressbook>mvn clean install
[INFO] Scanning for projects...
[WARNING]
[WARNING] Some problems were encountered while building the effective model for
com.packtpub.dynamodb.cookbook:addressbook:pom:1.0.0
[WARNING] 'modules.module[0]' has been specified without a path to the project d
irectory. @ line 17, column 11
[WARNING]
[WARNING] It is highly recommended to fix these problems because they threaten t
he stability of your build.
[WARNING]
[WARNING] For this reason, future Maven versions might no longer support buildin
g such malformed projects.
[WARNING]
[INFO] ------------------------------------------------------------------------
[INFO] Reactor Build Order:
[INFO]
[INFO] addressbook
[INFO] addressbook-services
[INFO] addressbook-controller Maven Webapp
[INFO]
[INFO] ------------------------------------------------------------------------
[INFO] Building addressbook 1.0.0
[INFO] ------------------------------------------------------------------------
[INFO]
```

2. Next, we need to make sure that all the required libraries are assembled in the war, so do the following setting for the the `addressbook-controller` project. Navigate to **project | Properties | Deployment Assembly | Add | Java Build Path Entries | Maven Dependencies**.

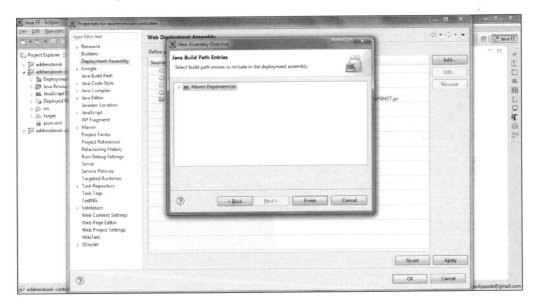

3. Now, we are all set to deploy our application. Right-click on the `addressbook-controller`, then navigate to **project | Amazon Web Services | Deploy to Elastic Beanstalk**.

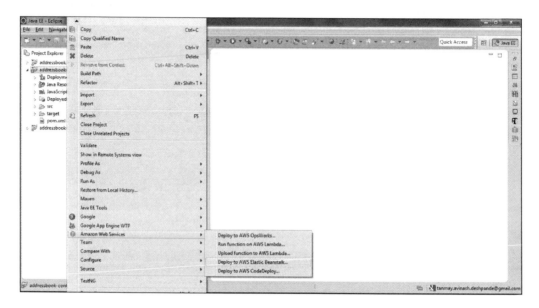

4. Now you will get an option to manually select the server on which you wish to deploy your application. Here, we will select **AWS Beanstalk for Tomcat8**:

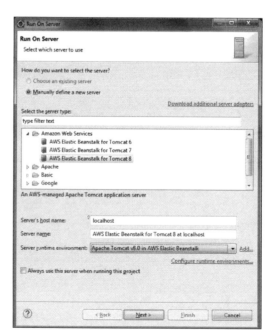

5. Click on **Next** to proceed. You will now see a window, which will ask you for the application and environment details. You can create multiple environments, such as the development, production, and so on. You also need to check whether you need a load balanced environment, or you just need a single instance. Here, we will select a single instance environment. You need to choose in which region you wish to deploy your application.

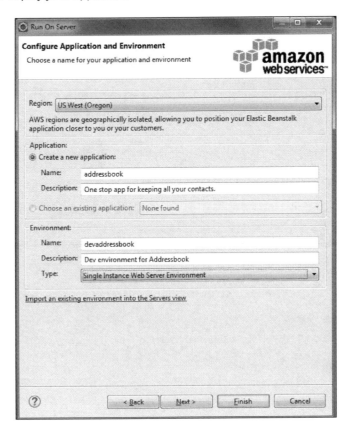

6. Next, you need to provide the advanced properties, and select the key with which you wish to deploy this app. Click on **Finish** to start the deployment.

7. On successful configuration, the plugin will contact AWS and will start the deployment process.

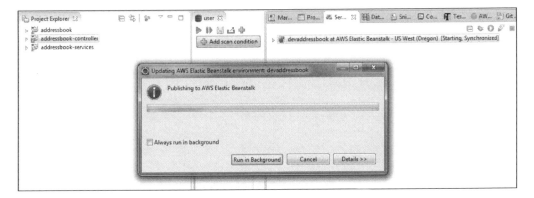

8. The deployment process generally takes time for completion. Meanwhile, you can go to the AWS Elastic Beanstalk console and track the progress from there.

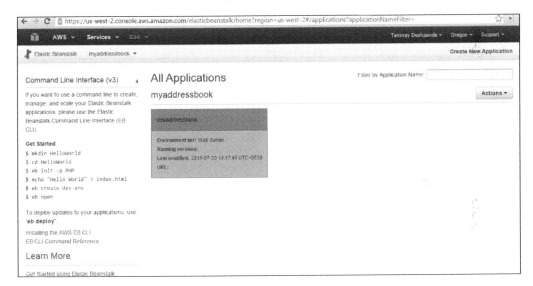

9. Once the deployment is complete, you can check whether the web app is up and running by hitting the app URL. On the the AWS Elastic Beanstalk console page, you will see the app in green color:

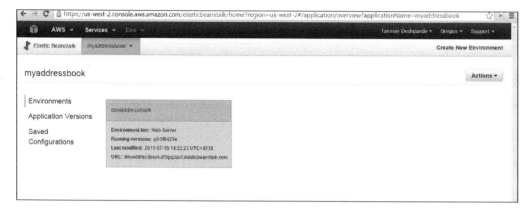

10. Now, we hit the URL to see our app up in running, for example, `http://devaddressbook-zf3gqzipxf.elasticbeanstalk.com/#/login`. For you, the URL can be different:

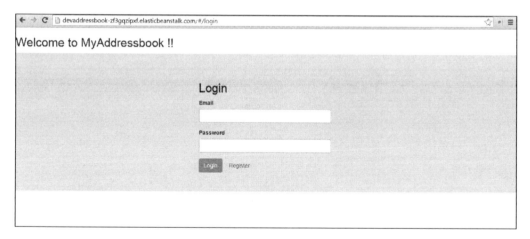

Try out operations such as register, login, add a new contact, view contacts, and so on:

11. Now, you can keep updating this app with more features, deploy it to new environments, and share it with your friends and colleagues. If you just want to learn, or in case, you don't want to keep this app running, you should terminate the environment from the AWS console.

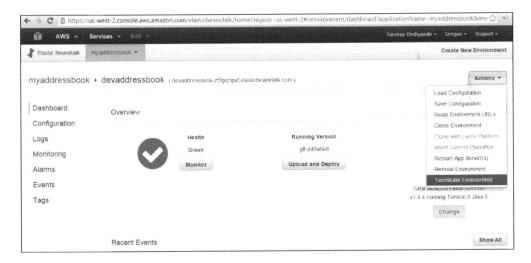

How it works...

Elastic Beanstalk is a platform as a service from Amazon Web Services. Here, when we deploy the environment, it first creates an AWS EC2 instance with an operating system of your choice. Once the instance is up and running, it installs the Tomcat web server on it. After the Tomcat installation, it takes our binaries and deploys the web application to Tomcat. If everything goes well, you should see your application up and running in Cloud within a few minutes.

For security purposes, it also creates the security groups and makes sure that the spawned EC2 instance is protected by policies applied on it. If you wish to add more security, you can go to the AWS EC2 instance console and apply the policies to the group.

This way, you have your end-to-end web application running in Cloud. Now, you can deploy any such application using AWS DynamoDB as the backend and make it scalable as required. Initially, if you have kept the provisioned throughput less, you can increase or decrease it as per the demand at any point of time, without taking down the application.

10
Developing Mobile Applications using DynamoDB

In this chapter, we will cover the following topics:

- ▶ Performing data modeling and table creation
- ▶ Creating an identity pool using AWS Cognito
- ▶ Creating the access policy and applying it to the AWS Cognito role
- ▶ Implementing user registration services
- ▶ Implementing user login services
- ▶ Implementing add new contact services
- ▶ Implementing view contacts services

Introduction

In the previous chapter, we discussed how to develop and deploy web applications using DynamoDB as a backend service. Now, it's time to understand how to use DynamoDB as a backend service for mobile applications.

In this chapter, we are going to create an Android app for an address book. For this, we will use DynamoDB as a backend service.

Steps to register and use the address book:

- A new user should be able to register to the application
- A registered user should be able to log in to the application
- A logged-in user should be able to add new contacts
- A logged-in user should be able to view the already added contacts

We would also like to see our application being installed on any Android device.

The technology stack for this application will be as follows:

- The Android SDK for service development
- DynamoDB for data storage

The complete code for this application is available for download at `https://github.com/deshpandetanmay/dynamodb-cookbook`.

Performing data modeling and table creation

In this recipe, we will see how to model data for this Android application and create DynamoDB tables accordingly.

Getting ready

To get started with this recipe, you need to know how to create a table in DynamoDB using the console.

How to do it...

To perform data modeling for any Android application using the NoSQL database as a backend, we need to first start with the queries, which we would like to execute on the tables. Considering the requirements, we will need at least two tables:

- **User**: This is a table used to store information of a valid user's details along with the credentials
- **Contact**: This is a table used to store information of all the contacts added by users

As we will be using the User table to save the registered user information, as well as to sign in, we can use an e-mail ID as a hash key for this table.

Here, we don't need a range key, as the e-mail ID being a primary hash key should be good enough to recognize a user for registration and login. So, let's create the `UserApp` table with `e-mail` as the hash key:

1. Log in to the AWS console and go to DynamoDB at `https://console.aws.amazon.com/dynamodb/`.

2. Create the `UserApp` table by providing the e-mail as the hash key and the data type as a String.

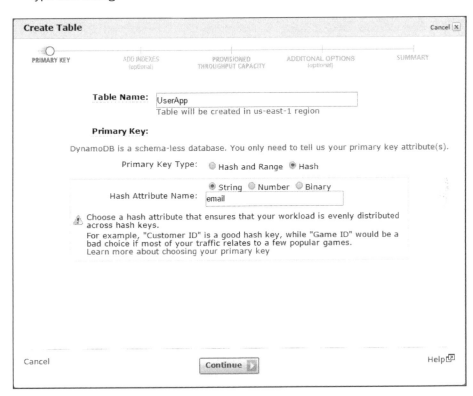

3. Here, we don't need to create any secondary indexes, so we can skip to the provisioned throughput page and give some numbers. As we are creating this app for learning purposes, we can keep the read and writes capacity units as 10 each. Now, proceed to complete the table creation process.

4. Next, we need to create the `ContactApp` table. This table will be used to store contacts for each registered user. So, we can create this table by providing the `contact id` as the hash key and `parentId` as the range key. Here, `parentId` can be an e-mail ID of a user to whom the contact belongs to.

5. Next, we click on **Continue** to proceed. Here, also, we don't need to create any secondary indexes, so we can skip to the provisioned throughput page. Here, we would be querying this table more than the `UserApp` table, so it's good to provide a healthy number for reads and writes. Let's say that we'll give 25 units to each. Proceed and complete the table creation.

How it works...

The strategy behind designing this schema is to provide an easy access to registration, login, and contact management services. Here, we choose an e-mail ID as the hash key, as we know that each user will have a unique e-mail ID, and this will also help you to distribute the data equally on DynamoDB partitions. DynamoDB automatically distributes the table data to multiple partitions. Here, the hash key plays an important role to decide in which partition an item would go. So, it's better to choose a primary key that will help in a unified data distribution across the partitions. Also, we can easily fetch the password for a given e-mail ID in order to verify the credentials.

In the `ContactApp` table, we will have the hash key as the contact ID and the range key as the e-mail ID of a user who added this contact. Here, we don't need to fetch contacts by their IDs, so we will use auto-generated values for this attribute. On the other hand, we will need to fetch all the contacts added by a specified user, which we can do using the range key.

Creating an identity pool using AWS Cognito

In the previous recipe, we created DynamoDB tables based on the need. Now, it's time to think of securely accessing DynamoDB from the Android app. Unlike what we did for web apps, here we cannot distribute the AWS secret key and access key with each app, as we need to distribute the app to a number of users. If we embed the access and secret keys in the **Android application package** (**APK**), then it will make our AWS environment vulnerable.

So, in order to solve this problem, AWS has launched a service called AWS Cognito, which is a great tool to provide limited/required access to app users. In this recipe, we are going to see how to use Cognito to create an identity pool. You can read about AWS Cognito at `https://aws.amazon.com/cognito/`.

Getting ready

To get started with this recipe, you need to know how to use the AWS console.

How to do it...

Let's create an identity pool using AWS Cognito:

1. Log in to the AWS web console and navigate to Cognito at `https://console.aws.amazon.com/cognito`.

    Click on the **Create new identity pool** button:

2. On clicking the button, you will see a page asking you for the details about the identity pool. You need to provide a valid name. Next, click on the unauthenticated identities checkbox so that we allow requests from various app users to have access to DynamoDB. There is another option from where you can choose to get the identity of users by asking the users to log in with their social accounts, such as Amazon, Facebook, Google+, Twitter, Open Id, or custom. You can read about the identity providers at `http://docs.aws.amazon.com/cognito/devguide/identity/external-providers/`.

   Click on **Create Pool** to continue.

3. Next, you will see a screen asking you to allow **Cognito** to access your resources. By default, it will create a new role and will assign the default policy to the new role. You can review the policy, and click on **Allow** if you are fine with the policy and the role:

4. On successful creation of the policy, role, and pool, you will see a page that will show you the sample code on how to use the identity in your program. From the drop-down menu, you can select the platform for which you need the sample. Here, we have selected Android, as we will develop an Android app. You also need to download the AWS SDK for Android by clicking on the given button. Make a note of the identity pool ID, and do not share it with anyone:

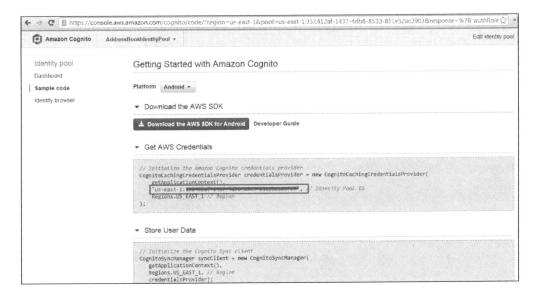

How it works...

Cognito creates the identity pools to keep track of requests using these pools. This is a better solution than providing app APKs with embedded secret and access keys. Here, we can choose what access the role will have for your infrastructure. This will also help you to understand the number of different users' identities. The dashboard will help you understand the number of identities created per day.

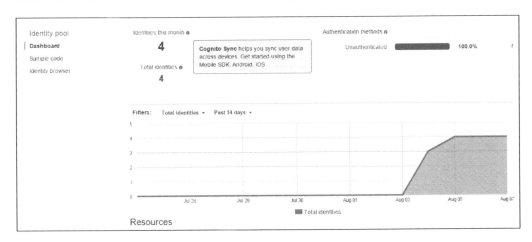

Creating the access policy and applying it to the AWS Cognito role

In the previous recipe, we created a role for the AWS Cognito identity pool. Now, it's time to create a policy and apply the role with the proper permissions for the Android app to access the required tables.

Getting ready

To get started with this recipe, you need to know how to use the AWS console.

How to do it...

Let's create a policy and apply the role:

1. Log in to the AWS web console and navigate to AWS IAM at `https://console.aws.amazon.com/iam/`.

2. Click on **Policies** and start creating a new policy. From the options, you can select **Create your own policy** and provide a policy document, as shown in the following code. Update only the AWS account number with your actual account number:

```json
{
    "Version": "2012-10-17",
    "Statement": [
        {
            "Effect": "Allow",
            "Action": [
                "dynamodb:DeleteItem",
                "dynamodb:GetItem",
                "dynamodb:PutItem",
                "dynamodb:Scan",
                "dynamodb:Query",
                "dynamodb:UpdateItem",
                "dynamodb:BatchWriteItem"
            ],
            "Resource": [
                "arn:aws:dynamodb:us-west-
                2:123445656:table/ContactApp/*",
                "arn:aws:dynamodb:us-west-
                2:112323334:table/UserApp/*"
            ]
        }
    ]
}
```

3. Now, click on the **Create Policy** button to proceed.

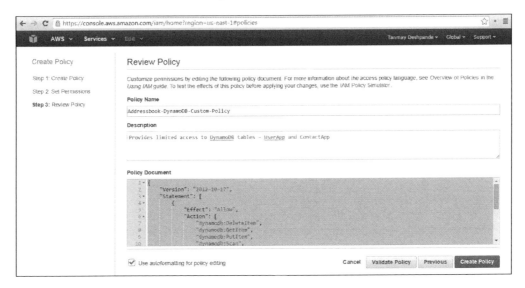

4. Now, it's time to move on to the Roles section to attach the created policy. From the list, select the `Cognito_AddressBookIdentityPoolUnauth_Role`, which was created when we created the identity pool. Click on the **Attach Policy** button, and select the policy that we created in the last step.

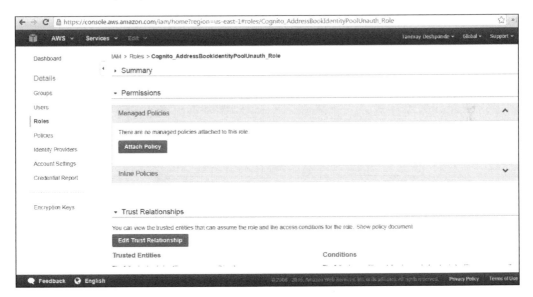

5. On successful application, you will see that the policy gets attached to the role.

How it works...

Cognito manages all the permissions for the identities in the identity pool by this role. By default, it does not give any permission to the app. So, we have to create a policy and apply it to this role so that any identity that comes from this pool should be able to access the required resources (for example, a DynamoDB table). If you take a look at the policy document carefully, you will notice that we only grant access to two tables for all item-level accesses. You can fine tune this in case you need to restrict users to certain permissions only.

Implementing user registration services

Now that we have set up all the required prerequisites for the Android app, it's time to start writing services for the user registration.

Getting ready...

To get started with this recipe, you need to have performed the earlier recipes and should have set up the Android application development kit either on Eclipse IDE or Android Studio. For more information, take a look at the following links:

▶ http://developer.android.com/sdk/installing/installing-adt.html
▶ http://developer.android.com/tools/studio/index.html

How to do it...

Let's implement user registration service:

1. To get started, we need to instantiate `AmazonDynamoDBClient` using the AWS Cognito identity pool, as follows:

```
CognitoCachingCredentialsProvider credentials = new
CognitoCachingCredentialsProvider(
    context, Constants.ACCOUNT_ID,
      Constants.IDENTITY_POOL_ID,
        Constants.UNAUTH_ROLE_ARN, null,
          Regions.US_EAST_1);
AmazonDynamoDBClient ddb = new
  AmazonDynamoDBClient(credentials);
ddb.setRegion(Region.getRegion(Regions.US_WEST_2));
```

Here, `Constants` is a static class that contains all the properties.

2. Next, we will use the object persistence model for DynamoDB, for which we will need to create a class for the user model:

```
@DynamoDBTable(tableName = Constants.USER_TABLE)
public static class AppUser {
    private String email;
    private String name;
    private String password;
    @DynamoDBHashKey
    public String getEmail() {
      return email;
    }
    public void setEmail(String email) {
      this.email = email;
    }
    @DynamoDBAttribute(attributeName = "name")
    public String getName() {
      return name;
    }
    public void setName(String name) {
      this.name = name;
    }
    @DynamoDBAttribute(attributeName = "password")
    public String getPassword() {
      return password;
```

```
    }
    public void setPassword(String password) {
      this.password = password;
    }
  }
```

This class will be used for both user registration and login.

3. Next, we need to write a method that will be called from on a register new user button click.

```
public static void register(AppUser appUser) {
  AmazonDynamoDBClient ddb = RegisterActivity.clientManager.ddb();
  DynamoDBMapper mapper = new DynamoDBMapper(ddb);
  try {
      Log.d(TAG, "Registering user");
      mapper.save(appUser);
      Log.d(TAG, "User inserted");
  } catch (AmazonServiceException ex) {
      Log.e(TAG, "Error inserting user");
    RegisterActivity.clientManager.wipeCredentialsOnAuthError(ex);
  }
}
```

4. While making any calls to DynamoDB, we need to use the `AsyncTask` executer services, and we should not call it directly from the UI thread; otherwise, you will get errors. Here is a sample `AsyncTask` that registers the user with our application by saving its details:

```
private class DynamoDBManagerTask extends
  AsyncTask<DynamoDBManagerType, Void, DynamoDBManagerTaskResult>
  {
    protected DynamoDBManagerTaskResult doInBackground(
      DynamoDBManagerType... types) {
    DynamoDBManagerTaskResult result = new
      DynamoDBManagerTaskResult();
    result.setTaskType(types[0]);
    if (types[0] == DynamoDBManagerType.INSERT_USER) {
      DynamoDBManager.register(user);
    }
    return result;
    }
    protected void onPostExecute(DynamoDBManagerTaskResult result)
  {
```

```
if (result.getTaskType() == DynamoDBManagerType.INSERT_USER) {
Toast.makeText(RegisterActivity.this,
"Registration Success!! Please Login.", Toast.LENGTH_SHORT)
  .show();
}
}
}
```

5. Once we integrate this with the UI, you will be able to see the registration process working smoothly.

How it works...

`DynamoDBMapper` is a class that helps us achieve the object persistence model of DynamoDB. This recipe focuses on how to integrate DynamoDB with Android. For details of the UI code, refer to `https://github.com/deshpandetanmay/dynamodb-cookbook`.

Implementing user login services

In this recipe, we are going to see how to implement login services for our Android app.

Getting ready...

To get started with this recipe, you need to have performed the earlier recipes and should have set up the Android application development kit either on Eclipse IDE or Android Studio. For more information, take a look at the following links:

- http://developer.android.com/sdk/installing/installing-adt.html
- http://developer.android.com/tools/studio/index.html

How to do it...

Let's implement user login services:

1. To provide login services to the user, we are going to use the same user model that which we created in the previous recipe. So, refer to the previous recipe for details on the `User` mode.

2. To log in, we will ask our user to enter the e-mail ID and password. So, our first task is to get a user by its e-mail ID. So, once we have the user details, we can validate the entered password with the password stored in the user table. So, let's write the method to get the user by its e-mail:

```
public static AppUser getUserByEmail(String email) {
AmazonDynamoDBClient ddb = LoginActivity.clientManager.ddb();
  DynamoDBMapper mapper = new DynamoDBMapper(ddb);
    try {
  AppUser appUser = mapper.load(AppUser.class, email);
    return appUser;
  } catch (AmazonServiceException ex) {
  LoginActivity.clientManager.wipeCredentialsOnAuthError
    (ex);
  }
  return null;
}
```

3. Once again, we will write the `AsyncTask` executor to avoid calling any DynamoDB-related service directly from the Android app UI:

```
private class DynamoDBManagerTask extends
  AsyncTask<DynamoDBManagerType, Void,
    DynamoDBManagerTaskResult> {
  protected DynamoDBManagerTaskResult doInBackground(
  DynamoDBManagerType... types) {
DynamoDBManagerTaskResult result = new
  DynamoDBManagerTaskResult();
  result.setTaskType(types[0]);
  if (types[0] == DynamoDBManagerType.GET_USER) {
  user = DynamoDBManager.getUserByEmail(email.getText()
```

```
      .toString());
      }
    return result;
    }
  // Validate password with entered password on post execute
  protected void onPostExecute(DynamoDBManagerTaskResult
    result) {
    if (result.getTaskType() == DynamoDBManagerType.GET_USER)
      {
      if (user.getPassword().equalsIgnoreCase(
        password.getText().toString())) {
          Toast.makeText(LoginActivity.this, "Login
            Successfull.", Toast.LENGTH_SHORT).show();
          redirectToActivity(null, HomeActivity.class);
      } else {
      Toast.makeText( LoginActivity.this,
        "Username or Password is incorrect.
          Please try again",
        Toast.LENGTH_SHORT).show();
      redirectToActivity(null, LoginActivity.class);
      }
    }
    }
    }
```

4. Here, if the password matches, then we redirect our user to the home screen, or else we keep the user on the login screen only. Here is a screenshot of the working Android app for the login UI:

On a successful login, you will see the home screen providing you with the options to view the already added contacts or add a new contact.

How it works...

`DynamoDBMapper` helps us fetch the user with the given hash key. Here, the e-mail ID is the hash key, so if the user exists, `DynamoDBMapper` will fetch the details. We can simply compare the password easily. Here, we are not storing the password in an encrypted manner as this is just a demo app for learning. If you need to use it for a production-level app, use the DynamoDB encryption library for encrypting the sensitive information.

Implementing add new contact services

In this recipe, we are going to see how to implement and add new contacts services to our Android app.

Getting ready...

To get started with this recipe, you should have performed the earlier recipes.

How to do it...

To save contacts against a specific user, we will use the `ContactApp` table, which we created earlier:

1. First of all, we need to define a model that we will use for various contact services. Here is our contact model:

```
@DynamoDBTable(tableName = Constants.CONTACT_TABLE)
  public static class AppContact {
    private String id;
    private String email;
    private String name;
    private String phone;
    private String parentId;
    public String getEmail() {
      return email;
    }
    public void setEmail(String email) {
      this.email = email;
    }
    @DynamoDBAttribute(attributeName = "name")
    public String getName() {
      return name;
    }
    public void setName(String name) {
      this.name = name;
    }
    @DynamoDBHashKey(attributeName = "id")
    @DynamoDBAutoGeneratedKey
    public String getId() {
      return id;
    }
    public void setId(String id) {
      this.id = id;
    }
    @DynamoDBAttribute(attributeName = "phone")
    public String getPhone() {
      return phone;
    }
```

```
    public void setPhone(String phone) {
      this.phone = phone;
    }
    @DynamoDBAttribute(attributeName = "parentId")
    @DynamoDBRangeKey
    public String getParentId() {
      return parentId;
    }
    public void setParentId(String parentId) {
      this.parentId = parentId;
    }
  }
```

Here, the attribute `id` is the hash key, while the `parentId` is the range key.
Here, `parentId` is nothing but the e-mail ID of the user who added this contact.

2. Next, we will write a method to add a new contact that is provided by a user in
   the DynamoDB table:

```
public static void addNewContact(AppContact appContact) {
AmazonDynamoDBClient ddb =
  ContactActivity.clientManager.ddb();
  DynamoDBMapper mapper = new DynamoDBMapper(ddb);
  try {
    Log.d(TAG, "Adding new contact");
    mapper.save(appContact);
    Log.d(TAG, "Contact saved");
  } catch (AmazonServiceException ex) {
    Log.e(TAG, "Error adding new contact");
      ContactActivity.clientManager
        .wipeCredentialsOnAuthError(ex);
  }
}
```

3. Next, we will integrate this method with the Android app UI to see the add new contact functionality working.

How it works...

In this case, we get contact-related information from the user, but we will also need to save which user added this contact. We save this information when a user logs in. We can do this using Android's shared preferences, which are like global variables and can used across the screens. We keep the user's e-mail in shared preferences of your Android app and fetch this information whenever needed. Here, again, we use the `DynamoDBMapper` class to persist the contact.

Implementing view contacts services

In this recipe, we are going to see how to implement view contacts services for our Android app.

Getting ready...

To get started with this recipe, you should have performed the earlier recipes.

How to do it...

Let's implement view contacts services:

1. To fetch the contacts saved by a particular user, we will use the same `AppContact` model that we used in the earlier recipe.

2. Next, we need to write a method that fetches all the contacts saved with a certain e-mail ID:

```
public static List<AppContact> getAllContacts(String email) {
AmazonDynamoDBClient ddb =
  ContactListActivity.clientManager.ddb();
    DynamoDBMapper mapper = new DynamoDBMapper(ddb);
    List<AppContact> contactList = new
      ArrayList<AppContact>();
    try {
      Log.d(TAG, "Fetching contacts");
    // Condition to get records for given userEmailId
      Condition condition = new
        Condition().withComparisonOperator(
          ComparisonOperator.EQ.toString())
            .withAttributeValueList(new AttributeValue()
              .withS(email));
      DynamoDBScanExpression scanExpression = new
        DynamoDBScanExpression();
      scanExpression.addFilterCondition("parentId",
        condition);
  // Paginated scan in case no. of contacts are too much
      PaginatedParallelScanList<AppContact> contacts = mapper
        .parallelScan(AppContact.class, scanExpression, 4);
      for (AppContact contact : contacts) {
      contactList.add(contact);
    }
    } catch (AmazonServiceException ex) {
    Log.e(TAG, "Error adding new contact");
```

```
ContactListActivity.clientManager
  .wipeCredentialsOnAuthError(ex);
}
return contactList;
}
```

3. Once we integrate this service with the Android app UI, we need to click on the **My Contacts** button, which will fetch all the contacts saved against a certain e-mail ID.

How it works...

Here, we are using a scan operation to scan all the contacts and filter only those records for a given range key. By doing this, we will be able to show you only those contacts that are added by the specific user. We will use a parallel scan operation in order to fetch the data quickly.

You can download the complete source code, update the values in the constants file with the account details, identity pool, and table names, and execute them on your machine/phone in order to see the app working. You can refer to the source code at https://github.com/deshpandetanmay/dynamodb-cookbook.

Index

Symbols

.zip format 21

A

access policy, for AWS Cognito role
  applying 222-224
  creating 222-224
add new contact services
  implementing 230-233
Address Book application
  services, developing for 200-206
Amazon DynamoDB. *See* DynamoDB
Android application package (APK) 219
asynchronous requests
  performing, to DynamoDB 153, 154
atomic transactions
  performing, on DynamoDB tables 151, 152
auto-retries
  about 150
  performing, on DynamoDB errors 148-150
AWS
  client errors 148
  server errors 148
AWS Billing FAQs
  URL 4
AWS CloudSearch
  about 181
  DynamoDB data, importing to 181-185
AWS CloudSearch console
  URL 182
AWS Cloud Trail
  about 174
  for logging DynamoDB operations 174-176

AWS Cognito
  about 219
  for creating identity pool 219-221
  URL 219
AWS Command Line Interface
  setting up, for DynamoDB 25-27
AWS Console
  URL 2
AWS Data Pipeline
  about 156
  URL 156
  used, for exporting data from AWS S3 to
      DynamoDB 159-163
  used, for importing data from AWS S3 to
      DynamoDB 156-159
AWS ElastiCache
  about 140
  using, for frequently accessed items 140-142
AWS Elastic Beanstalk
  about 206
  URL 206
  web applications, deploying on 206-214
AWS EMR
  for accessing DynamoDB data 163-167
  for exporting to AWS S3 from
      DynamoDB 172, 173
  for querying DynamoDB data 167-170
AWS IAM
  about 117
  URL 117
  used, for creating DynamoDB full
      access group 120-122
  used, for creating DynamoDB read-only
      group 122, 123

used, for creating fine-grained access
    control policy 129, 130
used, for creating users 118, 119
AWS IAM policy simulator
DynamoDB access controls, validating
    with 123-125
AWS Redshift
DynamoDB data, exporting to 176-181
prerequisites 176
AWS Redshift console
URL 177
AWS S3
about 145
URL 145
using, for storing large items 145, 146
AWS SDK, for Java
for creating DynamoDB table 32-34
for deleting DynamoDB table 42, 43
for listing DynamoDB tables 39, 40
for updating DynamoDB table 37
used, for creating DynamoDB table
    with GSI 76-78
used, for creating DynamoDB table
    with LSI 86-88
used, for deleting item from DynamoDB
    table 60, 61
used, for obtaining item from DynamoDB
    table 52
used, for obtaining multiple items from
    DynamoDB table 65, 66
used, for performing batch write
    operations 69, 70
used, for putting item into DynamoDB
    table 48, 49
used, for querying GSI 83, 84
used, for querying LSI 93, 94
used, for updating item from DynamoDB
    table 54-56
AWS SDK, for .Net
for creating DynamoDB table 34, 35
for deleting DynamoDB table 43, 44
for listing DynamoDB tables 40, 41
for updating DynamoDB table 38
multiple items, obtaining from DynamoDB
    table 66-68

used, for creating DynamoDB table
    with LSI 88-91
used, for deleting item from DynamoDB
    table 62
used, for obtaining item from
    DynamoDB table 52
used, for performing batch write
    operations 70-72
used, for putting item into DynamoDB
    table 50
used, for querying GSI 84, 85
used, for querying LSI 94
used, for updating item from DynamoDB
    table 56-58
AWS SDK, for .NET
used, for creating DynamoDB table
    with GSI 79, 80
AWS SDK, for PHP
for creating DynamoDB table 35, 36
for deleting DynamoDB table 44, 45
for listing DynamoDB tables 41, 42
for updating DynamoDB table 39
used, for creating DynamoDB table
    with GSI 81-83
used, for creating DynamoDB table
    with LSI 91-93
used, for deleting item from
    DynamoDB table 63, 64
used, for obtaining item from
    DynamoDB table 53
used, for obtaining multiple items from
    DynamoDB table 68, 69
used, for performing batch write
    operations 72, 73
used, for putting item into DynamoDB
    table 51
used, for querying GSI 85
used, for querying LSI 95
used, for updating item from DynamoDB
    table 58-60
AWS Toolkit, for Eclipse
URL 206

B

BatchGetItem operation 66-69

C

client-side encryption
  implementing, for DynamoDB data 131-134
client-side masking
  implementing, for DynamoDB data 134-136
CloudTrail event service
  reference 176
CloudWatch
  DynamoDB metric, analyzing on 17-20
custom object, for DynamoDB table
  creating, with object persistence model
    in Java 104-106
  creating, with object persistence model
    in .Net 112-114
custom policy
  creating 125-128

D

data
  accessing, AWS EMR used 163-167
  exporting from AWS S3 to DynamoDB,
    with AWS Data Pipeline 159-163
  exporting to AWS S3 from DynamoDB,
    with AWS EMR 172, 173
  importing from AWS S3 to DynamoDB, with
    AWS Data Pipeline 156-159
  querying, AWS EMR used 167-170
  querying, DynamoDB console used 11-15
data model, for DynamoDB item
  creating, with object persistence model in
    Java 100-102
data modeling
  performing 190-192, 216-218
data types
  document 9
  multi-valued 9
  scalar 9
DynamoDB
  about 1
  asynchronous requests,
    performing to 153, 154
DynamoDB access controls
  validating, with AWS IAM policy
    simulator 123-125

DynamoDB console
  signing up 2-4
DynamoDB data
  client-side encryption, implementing
    for 131-134
  client-side masking, implementing
    for 134-136
  exporting, to AWS Redshift 176-181
  full text search, performing with
    CloudSearch 185-188
  importing, to AWS CloudSearch 181-185
DynamoDB errors
  auto-retries, performing 148-150
  catching 147, 148
  reference 148
DynamoDB full access group
  creating, AWS IAM used 120-122
DynamoDB Local
  about 21
  downloading 21
  setting up 21, 22
DynamoDB Local JavaScript Shell
  using 23, 24
DynamoDBMapper 227
DynamoDB metric
  analyzing, on CloudWatch 17-20
DynamoDB operations
  logging, AWS Cloud Trail used 174-176
DynamoDB read-only group
  creating, AWS IAM used 122, 123
DynamoDB table
  atomic transactions, performing 151, 152
  batch write operations, performing with AWS
    SDK for Java 69, 70
  batch write operations, performing with AWS
    SDK for .Net 70-72
  batch write operations, performing with AWS
    SDK for PHP 72, 73
  creating, AWS SDK for Java used 32-34
  creating, AWS SDK for .Net used 34, 35
  creating, AWS SDK for PHP used 35, 36
  creating, console used 4-9
  creating with Global Secondary Index, AWS
    SDK for Java used 76-78
  creating with Global Secondary Index, AWS
    SDK for .Net used 79, 80

creating with Global Secondary Index, AWS
SDK for PHP used 81

creating with Local Secondary Index, AWS
SDK for Java used 86-88

creating with Local Secondary Index, AWS
SDK for .Net used 88-90

creating with Local Secondary Index, AWS
SDK for PHP used 91-93

data loading, console used 9, 10

deleting, AWS SDK for Java used 42, 43

deleting, AWS SDK for .Net used 43, 44

deleting, AWS SDK for PHP used 44, 45

deleting, console used 15-17

item, deleting with AWS SDK for Java 60, 61

item, deleting with AWS SDK for .Net 62

item, deleting with AWS SDK for PHP 63, 64

item, obtaining with AWS SDK for Java 52

item, obtaining with AWS SDK for .Net 52

item, obtaining with AWS SDK for PHP 53

items, putting with AWS SDK for Java 48, 49

items, putting with AWS SDK for .Net 50

items, putting with AWS SDK for PHP 51

item, updating with AWS SDK for Java 54-56

item, updating with AWS SDK for .Net 56, 57

item, updating with AWS SDK for PHP 58-60

listing, AWS SDK for Java used 39, 40

listing, AWS SDK for .Net used 40, 41

listing, AWS SDK for PHP used 41, 42

multiple items, obtaining with AWS SDK
for Java 65, 66

multiple items, obtaining with AWS SDK
for .Net 66-68

multiple items, obtaining with AWS SDK
for PHP 68, 69

updating, AWS SDK for Java used 37

updating, AWS SDK for .Net used 38

updating, AWS SDK for PHP used 39

E

Eclipse IDE
setting up 27-29
EhCache
about 140
URL 138

F

fine-grained access control policy
creating, AWS IAM used 129, 130
First In First Out (FIFO) 140
frequently accessed items
AWS ElastiCache, using for 140-142
standalone cache, using for 138-140

G

Global Secondary Index (GSI)
about 76
querying, AWS SDK for Java used 83, 84
querying, AWS SDK for .Net used 84, 85
querying, AWS SDK for PHP used 85, 86
used, for quick lookups 96, 97

I

identity pool
creating, AWS Cognito used 219-221
identity providers
URL 220
items
putting, into DynamoDB table with object
persistence model in Java 102, 103
querying, from DynamoDB table with object
persistence model in Java 106, 107
querying, from DynamoDB table with object
persistence model in .Net 114
retrieving, from DynamoDB table with object
persistence model in Java 103, 104
retrieving, from DynamoDB table with object
persistence model in .Net 111
saving, into DynamoDB table with object
persistence model in .Net 109, 110
scanning, from DynamoDB table with object
persistence model in Java 108, 109
scanning, from DynamoDB table with object
persistence model in .Net 115

J

Java Archive (JAR) file 21
Java Cryptography Extension (JCE)
URL 134

Java Runtime Engine (JRE) 21
join operations
  performing on DynamoDB data,
      AWS EMR used 171, 172

L

large data
  compressing 142-144
Least Recently Used (LRU) 140
Local Secondary Index (LSI)
  about 76
  querying, AWS SDK for Java used 93, 94
  querying, AWS SDK for .Net used 94
  querying, AWS SDK for PHP used 95

M

Memcached
  URL 140

P

Postman rest client
  URL 196
PutItem API
  references 51, 52

Q

Query operation 15

R

Redis
  URL 140

S

Scan operation 15
services
  developing, for Address Book
      application 200-205
  developing, for sign-in activity for web
      applications 198-200
  developing, for sign-up activity for web
      applications 193-197

Social Security number (SSN) 134
Spring MVC
  URL 196
standalone cache
  using, for frequently accessed items 138-140

T

table creations
  performing 190-218
tar.gz format 21

U

user login services
  implementing 227-230
user registration services
  implementing 224-227
users
  creating, AWS IAM used 118, 119

V

view contacts services
  implementing 234, 235

W

web applications
  deploying, on AWS Elastic Beanstalk 206-214

Thank you for buying
DynamoDB Cookbook

About Packt Publishing

Packt, pronounced 'packed', published its first book, *Mastering phpMyAdmin for Effective MySQL Management*, in April 2004, and subsequently continued to specialize in publishing highly focused books on specific technologies and solutions.

Our books and publications share the experiences of your fellow IT professionals in adapting and customizing today's systems, applications, and frameworks. Our solution-based books give you the knowledge and power to customize the software and technologies you're using to get the job done. Packt books are more specific and less general than the IT books you have seen in the past. Our unique business model allows us to bring you more focused information, giving you more of what you need to know, and less of what you don't.

Packt is a modern yet unique publishing company that focuses on producing quality, cutting-edge books for communities of developers, administrators, and newbies alike. For more information, please visit our website at www.packtpub.com.

Writing for Packt

We welcome all inquiries from people who are interested in authoring. Book proposals should be sent to author@packtpub.com. If your book idea is still at an early stage and you would like to discuss it first before writing a formal book proposal, then please contact us; one of our commissioning editors will get in touch with you.

We're not just looking for published authors; if you have strong technical skills but no writing experience, our experienced editors can help you develop a writing career, or simply get some additional reward for your expertise.

MasteringDynamoDB

ISBN: 978-1-78355-195-8   Paperback: 236 pages

Master the intricacies of the NoSQL database DynamoDB to take advantage of its fast performance and seamless scalability

1. Implement DynamoDB as a backend to your iOS and Android mobile applications.

2. Explore how DynamoDB can be integrated with other AWS offerings such as EMR, Redshift, Cloudsearch, and more.

3. Equip yourself with best practices to improve the time and cost performance of your application through interactive tutorials.

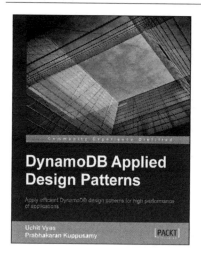

DynamoDB Applied Design Patterns

ISBN: 978-1-78355-189-7   Paperback: 202 pages

Apply efficient DynamoDB design patterns for high performance of applications

1. Create, design, and manage databases in DynamoDB.

2. Immerse yourself in DynamoDB design examples and user cases, be it for new users or expert ones.

3. Perform sharding and modeling, to give your applications the low cost NoSQL edge.

Please check **www.PacktPub.com** for information on our titles

PUBLISHING

Amazon Web Services: Migrating your .NET Enterprise Application

Evaluate your Cloud requirements and successfully migrate your .NET Enterprise application to the Amazon Web Services Platform

Rob Linton [PACKT] enterprise

Amazon Web Services: Migrating your .NET Enterprise Application

ISBN: 978-1-84968-194-0   Paperback: 336 pages

Evaluate your Cloud requirements and successfully migrate your .NET Enterprise application to the Amazon Web Services Platform

1. Get to grips with Amazon Web Services from a Microsoft Enterprise .NET viewpoint.

2. Fully understand all of the AWS products including EC2, EBS, and S3.

3. Quickly set up your account and manage application security.

4. Learn through an easy-to-follow sample application with step-by-step instructions.

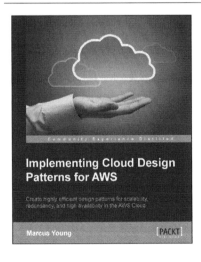

Implementing Cloud Design Patterns for AWS

Create highly efficient design patterns for scalability, redundancy, and high availability in the AWS Cloud

Marcus Young [PACKT]

Implementing Cloud Design Patterns for AWS

ISBN: 978-1-78217-734-0   Paperback: 228 pages

Create highly efficient design patterns for scalability, redundancy, and high availability in the AWS Cloud

1. Create highly robust systems using cloud infrastructure.

2. Make web applications resilient against scheduled and accidental down-time.

3. Explore and apply Amazon-provided services in unique ways to solve common problems.

Please check **www.PacktPub.com** for information on our titles